D1444368

THE HAYMARKET SQUARE RIOT TRIAL

A Headline Court Case

Headline Court Cases

THE HAYMARKET SQUARE RIOT TRIAL

A Headline Court Case

Bryna J. Fireside

E **Enslow Publishers, Inc.**

40 Industrial Road   PO Box 38
Box 398   Aldershot
Berkeley Heights, NJ 07922 Hants GU12 6BP
USA   UK

http://www.enslow.com

In memory of Alice Hansen Cook

The author would like to thank
Professor Jeff Cowie of Cornell University;
Les Orear, president of the Illinois Labor History Society;
and her husband, Harvey Fireside.

Copyright © 2002 by Bryna J. Fireside

Library of Congress Cataloging-in-Publication Data

Fireside, Bryna J.
  The Haymarket Square riot trial : a headline court case / Bryna J. Fireside.
    p. cm. – (Headline court cases)
Includes bibliographical references and index.
  ISBN 0-7660-1761-3
1. Trials (Anarchy)—Illinois—Chicago—Juvenile literature. 2. Haymarket Square Riot,
Chicago, Ill., 1886—Juvenile literature. I. Title. II. Series.
  KF223.H3774 F57 2002
  345.73'0243—dc21
                        2001004334

Printed in the United States of America

10 9 8 7 6 5 4 3 2 1

To Our Readers:
We have done our best to make sure that all Internet Addresses in this book were active
and appropriate when we went to press. However, the author and publisher have no control over and assume no liability for the material available on those Internet sites or on
other Web sites they may link to. Any comments or suggestions can be sent by e-mail to
comments@enslow.com or to the address on the back cover.

Illustration Credits: Dover Publications, pp. 7, 37; Historic Pullman Foundation,
p. 21; Illinois Labor History Society, pp. 3, 14, 40, 48, 52, 62, 68, 73, 79, 82, 86, 98, 101,
104, 106; Library of Congress, pp. 17, 34, 109; National Archives, pp. 31, 89.

Cover Illustration: Library of Congress. This is an artist's depiction of the Haymarket
Square Riot. Later evidence showed that most (if not all) of the gunshots came from the
police, not civilians.

Contents

Author's Note

Someone threw a bomb on the night of May 4, 1886. It instantly killed Police Officer Mathias Degan and injured scores of other police officers who had come to stop a labor protest rally. Mayor Carter Harrison knew of the meeting and made no effort to prevent it. It happened in the city of Chicago, Illinois, some time after 10:00 P.M. The rally had been called to protest the killing of several workers at the McCormick Harvester factory the day before. It was winding down when more than one hundred police officers arrived to disperse the people gathered. After the explosion, shooting erupted and both civilians and police officers were wounded or killed. In all, seven police officers died. No one ever found out how many civilians died. This was the Haymarket Square Riot.

Although the violence lasted no more than ten minutes, newspaper accounts led the public to believe that the city was on the verge of a violent revolution at the hands of foreign radicals. It was the first "red scare" in the United States. It was the first real fear of a communist takeover the country had ever known.

Eight men were tried for conspiracy to commit murder. All were found guilty, even though the person who actually threw the bomb was never found, and even though virtually all of the shots fired came from the police.

This was a dark period in the history of the United States. It was a period in which the newspapers and a small number of wealthy businesspeople led ordinary people to believe the city of Chicago was on the verge of a violent

In the nineteenth and early twentieth centuries, workers were not protected by law from poor conditions and inadequate pay. Members of this family, including the small children, worked for many hours each day making artificial flowers.

revolution—all due to a handful of people whose aim was to improve the lives of workers.

Today, we take certain working conditions for granted: A minimum wage, unemployment insurance, social security, safe working conditions, worker's compensation should a person be injured on the job, the eight-hour workday, and extra pay for overtime are all standard. In 1886 none of these things was available to the workers.

At the time, few people questioned the fact that none of the eight men who were put on trial for conspiracy to commit murder had been proven to have actually thrown the bomb. Few people gave thought to the fact that several of the men on trial were not even present at the Haymarket rally when the bomb went off. People wanted to see those responsible for the death of Officer Degan, six other police officers who died later, and the eighty police officers wounded by gunfire on the night of May 4, 1886, brought to justice. But there were many people who wanted something more. They wanted to silence the rally organizers (who happened to be anarchists) forever. They wanted no more talk of workers' rights, and no more talk about such "un-American" ideas as communism, anarchism, or socialism. The trial of the anarchists was partly a test of the First Amendment to the U.S. Constitution. It says, "Congress shall make no law respecting an establishment of religion, or prohibiting the freedom of speech, or of the press, or the right of people peaceably to assemble and to petition the Government for a redress of grievances."

It would take an honest governor to speak the truth and act courageously several years after the trial—after four men had already been hanged and a fifth had taken his own life.

Who's Who in the Haymarket Trial

William P. Black. Defense attorney for the accused. Civil War veteran usually addressed as "Captain Black."

Captain John Bonfield. Inspector, Chicago Police Department. He ordered police to break up the protest rally at Haymarket Square after Mayor Harrison told him not to send his men there.

Mathias Degan. A police officer killed by the bomb.

George Engel. Defendant. He had not actually attended the rally.

Samuel Fielden. Defendant.

Adolph Fischer. Defendant.

Judge Joseph Gary. Judge who presided over the trial of the anarchists.

Julius S. Grinnell. Illinois State's Attorney in Chicago. Prosecutor.

Carter H. Harrison. Mayor of Chicago. Testified that the rally had been peaceful. Ordered Captain Bonfield not to send his troops in.

Paul Hull. Reporter for *Chicago Daily News*. Testified for the prosecution.

George C. Ingham. Chief assistant to prosecutor.

Louis Lingg. Defendant. He did not attend the rally.

Oscar Neebe. Defendant. He did not attend the rally.

Albert Richard Parsons. The only American-born defendant.

Moses Salomon. Assistant to Captain Black.

Captain Schaack. Police officer who paid Seliger and Waller money to testify against defendants.

Rudolph Schnaubelt. Formally charged as the person who threw the bomb, but fled Chicago and never returned.

Michael Schwab. Defendant. He did not attend the rally.

William Seliger. Was arrested, but never formally charged because he provided evidence for the prosecution.

August Spies. Defendant.

Gottfried Waller. Arrested and charged. Provided evidence for the prosecution.

chapter one

A GREAT TRAGEDY

LABOR RALLY—About twenty-five hundred people gathered at Haymarket Square, a vegetable market west of downtown Chicago, on the evening of May 4, 1886. A rally had been called by a group of well-known anarchists to protest the killing of six workers who had been on strike against the McCormick Harvester factory the day before. A strike is a withholding of labor as a bargaining tool. It is a way to protest unfair working conditions. The men at the McCormick factory were killed by the Chicago police. The men who were killed were among thousands of workers who had been on strike for the past two months. They had formed a union so they could bargain with the owners of the factory for shorter hours and better wages. A union is a group of individuals who come together to achieve better working conditions. The factory owners locked the strikers out and hired nonunion workers to replace them.[1] The factory owners

11

refused to recognize the workers' union, and the men walked off the job. Trouble erupted when the men on strike threw stones at the men who had taken their jobs. The people who were hired to replace the striking workers were called "scabs."

As the scabs came out of the factory at the end of their shift, the men on strike shouted at them, calling them names. They threw rocks and stones and forced the scabs back inside the factory. When the police arrived, shots were fired. One newspaper reported that six strikers had died, and many more were wounded.

According to the *Chicago Herald,* "one hundred police officers were placed on either side of the 'scabs,'" and they were escorted to their homes.[2]

August Spies, the editor of the German-language newspaper, the *Arbeiter-Zeitung,* arrived at the scene just after the striking workers were fired on. Spies had been speaking to another group of strikers, members of the Lumber Shovers Union, when he heard the shots. He rushed back to his newspaper office and wrote a stinging one-page circular in both German and English. It came out with the headline:

"REVENGE! WORKINGMEN! TO ARMS!" The word "revenge" had been mistakenly inserted by the person who typed the circular (not Spies), but it would soon be used against Spies. There was more inflammatory language in the circular, in which Spies called workers "To arms, we call you, to arms!"[3]

Meanwhile, groups of workers in the city were meeting to see what action could be taken to protest the killings of the McCormick factory workers. One of the groups that held a meeting was the *Lehr-und-Wehr-Verein* (Instruction and Protection Society). This was a group of German socialists who formed a self-defense organization. They armed themselves and met to practice how to protect the workers. They wore blue uniforms, and during parades supporting workers, they marched with their guns and bayonets.

Adolph Fischer, who also worked at the paper, had already created a flyer to be given out to union members throughout Chicago. Its last line said, "Workingmen Arm Yourselves and Appear in Full Force!"

Several hundred copies of the flyer had already been printed before August Spies saw the last line. He demanded that it be taken out. "I objected to that line," he said, "as ridiculous to put in a phrase which would prevent people from attending the meeting."[4] Fischer agreed with him, and twenty thousand flyers were printed without those disturbing words.

However, copies of the original flyer fell into the hands of the police. Inspector John Bonfield, who was in charge of the "flying patrol wagon," a sort of nineteenth-century SWAT team, was at the nearby Des Plaines Police Station. He gave orders to his men to arm themselves and to be ready to break up a demonstration if it turned violent.

Despite the twenty thousand flyers without the inflammatory message, fewer than three thousand people actually showed up that evening. It was a chilly night, and the rally was late in getting started. Even some of the speakers arrived late.

Attention Workingmen!

GREAT
MASS-MEETING

TO-NIGHT, at 7.30 o'clock,
AT THE
HAYMARKET, Randolph St., Bet. Desplaines and Halsted.

Good Speakers will be present to denounce the latest atrocious act of the police, the shooting of our fellow-workmen yesterday afternoon.

Workingmen Arm Yourselves and Appear in Full Force!
THE EXECUTIVE COMMITTEE.

Achtung Arbeiter!

Große
Massen-Versammlung

Heute Abend, halb 8 Uhr, auf dem
Heumarkt, Randolph-Straße, zwischen Desplaines- u. Halsted-Str.

Gute Redner werden den neuesten Schurkenstreich der Polizei, indem sie gestern Nachmittag unsere Brüder erschoß, geißeln.

Arbeiter, bewaffnet Euch und erscheint massenhaft!
Das Executiv-Comite.

THE CALL FOR THE HAYMARKET MEETING.—I.
Photographic Engraving, direct from the Original.

The flyer announcing the meeting at Haymarket Square was printed in English and German. August Spies objected to the line, "Workingmen Arm Yourselves and Appear in Full Force," so it was removed, but not before several hundred flyers had been printed.

Different speakers made different points about the violence that had occurred the day before. Organizer August Spies blamed the deaths of the striking workers on the factory owners, the Chicago police, private detectives, and the strikebreakers (scabs).

Albert Parsons, one of the best-known leaders of the socialists of Chicago, told the crowd that instead of getting "ten hours' pay for eight hours' work, statistics proved that workingmen today were getting only two hours' pay for ten hours' work."[5] In other words, even if workers convinced the factory owners to give them the eight-hour workday, they still would be getting paid for only a couple of hours of work.

Samuel Fielden, who was described by the *Chicago Herald* as "a grim-visaged anarchist, wearing a black slouch hat,"[6] told the crowd that people like himself "were willing to risk their lives for the cause. It was," he said, "a glorious death to die like a hero rather than be starved to death on 60 cents a day."[7] (Words such as "anarchist," "socialist," "communist," "agitator," and "foreigner," were used interchangeably by the newspapers at that time.)

The mayor of Chicago, Carter H. Harrison, went to the rally at around 9:00 P.M. "I went down to the meeting and mingled with the crowd, going from point to point, hearing all that was said. . . . The crowd did not strike me as being sympathetic with the speakers."[8] In fact, Harrison told reporters that while people who were standing near the speakers applauded loudly and cheered them, those who were standing farther away complained that those men "never work!" Convinced that the rally was not going to be dangerous, the mayor left. He went to the Des Plaines Police Station and instructed Inspector Bonfield *not* to send the police out to the rally. Then he went home.

But Bonfield ignored the mayor's orders. At around 10:00 P.M. he led nearly two hundred police officers to the Haymarket site.

By this time it was raining and a chilly wind had kicked up. There were fewer than four hundred people still standing around. The last speaker, Samuel Fielden, was finishing his speech. He was about to tell everyone to go home.

Captain William Ward, who led the first platoon of police, demanded that the rally disband immediately. "I command you, in the name of the people of the state of Illinois, immediately and peaceably to disperse!"[9]

Fielden was surprised. "But we are peaceable," he protested.[10] Captain Ward repeated his command.

"All right, we will go," said Fielden, and he stepped down from the wagon from which they were speaking.

Suddenly, there was a terrible explosion! Someone had thrown a homemade bomb into the gathering of police officers. Officer Mathias Degan was immediately killed. Newspapers reported that six other police officers died later. In the confusion that followed, shots were fired, killing and wounding police and demonstrators. No one was sure how many demonstrators died or were wounded, because their friends removed their bodies. It was reported that more than seventy-five police officers were wounded either by gunfire or by flying objects. The violence lasted only ten minutes.

There was such confusion, as the police tried to save their own men, that no arrests were actually made that night.

This was the first time in American history that a dynamite bomb was exploded at a demonstration. No one knew who had made it or who had thrown it.

The next day, the newspapers were filled with vivid stories of the horror of the night before. The *Chicago Tribune* described in detail the scene at Haymarket Square and at the Des Plaines Police Station, as bleeding and wounded officers were brought into the station house. Unnamed reporters claimed that there were "enthusiastic Germans . . . and [a] large number of Poles and Bohemians, besides some American-looking people who came to look

The Haymarket Riot, May 4, 1886. The artist's drawing shows guns being fired by both police and civilians, but later evidence suggests that most (if not all) of the shots came from the police.

on. . . ."[11] One reporter wrote that he heard three men discussing anticipated trouble.

> Several men, had their revolvers in their hands under their coats and were prepared for an attack. . . . The [quickness] with which the leaders of the [bombing] got out of the way as soon as the explosion occurred was a little short of marvelous, and this fact led many to believe that they had knowledge of what was to be done, and therefore took occasion to escape the consequences they knew would follow.[12]

In the days that followed, the police searched the homes and offices of labor activists. They were looking for evidence of bomb-making equipment. Each day the headlines in newspapers called for vengeance against the anarchists. One headline said, "Now it is Blood! A Bomb Thrown into [Police] Ranks Inaugurates The Work of Death."[13]

What Is

An anarchist? Someone who believes that people can govern themselves without intervention by the government.

A communist? Someone who believes that private ownership of the means of production should be abolished.

A radical? Someone who wants to make fundamental changes to the existing order.

A socialist? Someone who believes in government ownership of factories and thinks that goods should be distributed according to work done.

The police arrested more than one hundred thirty people. All but seven people were eventually released. One man, Albert Parsons, fled to another state but returned to stand trial with the others. Another, Rudolph Schnaubelt, left the city and was never heard from again. Several men who were charged by the prosecution with "conspiracy to destroy the city" had not even been at the Haymarket rally at the time of the explosion. Yet, when a person is charged with conspiracy, he or she does not have to actually be the person to have committed a crime. It is enough to have known about a crime and to have helped it happen in some way.

By the time eight men were formally charged, people all over the country were calling for the death of the anarchists. Many people feared that a revolution was about to begin. Their fears were heightened by vivid newspaper accounts, many of which were less than factual. Many people believed that unless the leaders of the demonstration were put on trial and punished, anarchy would take over.

chapter two

EVENTS LEADING UP TO THE HAYMARKET RIOT

DEPRESSION—By 1873 there was an "economic downturn," or a depression, throughout the United States. There was a great deal of unemployment. The average yearly income of eleven million of the nation's twelve million working families had dwindled to just $380. Yet it was estimated that it took a yearly wage of $506 for the head of a household to keep his family out of poverty.[1] When a man lost his job, life was uncertain. There was nothing in place, such as unemployment insurance, to help an unemployed worker over a difficult time. Men who left home to look for work in other cities were called tramps.

At the same time, there were a few people accumulating great wealth, as never before in our history. Many of them lived in a lavish style. Mrs. Stuyvesant Fish, for example, whose husband owned the Illinois Central Railroad, threw a dinner party at a fancy New York restaurant to honor her dog. The dog arrived wearing a diamond collar worth $15,000![2] In fact, a tiny number of people, one

In the 1880s, wealth was concentrated among a few Americans, some of whom had very lavish lifestyles. Shown are the industrialist George Pullman and his wife, Harriet, who lived in a Chicago mansion that contained a pipe organ and a small theater.

percent of Americans, owned more than half the property in our country. And a mere 2 percent of the population received more than half of the income from all sources.[3]

After the Civil War ended in 1865, America became "a paradise of freebooting capitalists, untrammeled and untaxed. They [the capitalists] demanded always a free hand in the market, promising that in enriching themselves, they would 'build up the country' for the benefit of all the peoples."[4]

The government was eager to forget the Civil War years. Presidents, members of Congress, and judges embraced the capitalists with open arms, and often with open palms. For example, The Homestead Act of 1862 gave 160 acres of land to farmers and settlers. The land was free for those who lived on it for five years, and $1.25 an acre for those who lived on it for six months. Although many individuals did settle our western states in this manner, the Homestead Act actually worked in favor of cattle ranchers and railroad speculators (those who hoped to make a lot of money by owning the most land). Two hundred seventy million acres of land ended up in the hands of cattle ranchers and railroad speculators. Two hundred million acres went to the railroad speculators alone. The men who owned the railroads (built on land they grabbed from the American people) believed that they were somehow chosen by God to rule over workingmen and workingwomen everywhere. After a long strike against the Philadelphia & Reading Mining Company, owner George F. Baer wrote to the miners:

. . . the rights and interests of the laboring man will be protected and cared for by the Christian men to whom God has given control of the property rights of the country. Pray earnestly that right may triumph, always remember that the Lord God Omnipotent still reigns.[5]

These wealthy men did not seem to care that the money they paid their workers was so little that families were starving while they paid themselves salaries in the millions. These men, whose names are still familiar to us today— John D. Rockefeller, Andrew Mellon, J. P. Morgan, Jay Gould, and others—had little regard for the well-being of ordinary people. Jay Gould, owner of railroads, is said to have boasted that he could "hire one half of the working class to kill the other half."[6] These men, and others like them, were given the name "Robber Barons" by the embattled farmers of Kansas "who were being stripped of their livelihood by the owners of the Railroads who charged them so much money to ship their produce to market, that the farmers, themselves, were close to starvation."[7]

The arrogance of these barons of industry was best described by Robert Townsend Martin in his book *The Passing of the Idle Rich* in 1912:

We care not for politicians or public thinkers; we are the rich; we own America; we got it, God knows how; but we intend to keep it if we can by throwing all the tremendous weight of our support, our influence, our money, our political connections, our purchased senators, our hungry congressmen, our public-speaking demagogues into the scale against any legislators, any political platform, and Presidential campaign, that threatens the integrity of our estate.[8]

Events Leading Up to the Haymarket Riot

1868—Congress approves the eight-hour workday for all federal workers. It is not mandatory, however, and very few workplaces comply.

1870—The United States experiences an economic depression. Workers organize into unions to fight for jobs and better wages. Unions are ruled illegal in most states.

October 8–11, 1871—The Great Chicago Fire leaves 100,000 people homeless. Seventy-three miles of streets are destroyed. Some 17,500 buildings are destroyed. Estimated loss to the city is almost $200 million.

December 23, 1873—"Bread riots" occur in Chicago. Some 20,000 people march to City Hall to demand bread, clothing, and shelter.

May 1877—Pennsylvania Railroad announces a 10 percent cut in wages for all workers.

July 16, 1877—B & O Railroad announces a 10 percent wage cut. Workers call a strike and walk off the job in Camden Junction, Maryland. The strike spreads to West Virginia, Kentucky, and Ohio.

July 23, 1877—The railroad strike reaches Chicago. Twenty-five thousand people walk off their jobs as the railroad strike becomes a spark for many strikes by many different workers. Albert Parsons addresses the crowd and tells them "never to attack anyone unless they are attacked."[9]

July 25, 1877—Police clash with strikers when strikers taunt a group of scabs. Eighty thousand strikers destroy two locomotives. Police kill three people and wound seven. Workers all across Chicago put down their tools and join the railroad workers' strike.

July 27, 1877—The strike is crushed when private detectives, Civil War veterans, and state militias are called out. A dozen men are killed and dozens more are wounded. All of the dead are civilians.[10]

1882—Chicago bricklayers, tanners, and furriers go on strike.

1883—Telegraph workers strike for shorter hours and higher pay. The International Working People's Association (IWPA) is formed in Chicago.

1884—The Central Labor Union is formed in Chicago. Twenty-two trade unions join, including cigar makers, butchers, painters, printers, metal workers, cabinetmakers, and others. Seventy-six percent of Chicago's population is listed as foreign-born.[11]

1885—Metal workers in Chicago form an armed group after they clash with police and private detectives in April.[12]

July 2, 1885—Streetcar workers strike. Captain John Bonfield of the Chicago Police Department hits innocent people with his club, including a sixty-five-year-old man waiting for a wagon ride downtown.[13]

September 15, 1885—*Chicago Daily News* publishes articles about the corruption in the Des Plaines

Police Department. Commanding officers there are Bonfield and Ward. No one investigates the charges.

1886—The Illinois Bureau of Labor Statistics reports factory workers in Chicago earned less than they had in 1882—$2.00 a day for men; $1.11 a day for women; and 70 cents a day for children. Workers worked only 37.1 weeks on average that year.

May 1, 1886—Eighty thousand striking workers, led by Albert and Lucy Parsons and their children, march down Michigan Avenue in downtown Chicago to demand an eight-hour workday. There are no reports of violence.

May 3, 1886—Lizzie Holmes and Lucy Parsons lead a march of several hundred seamstresses through the streets of Chicago, demanding an eight-hour work-day. Chicago police shoot and kill striking workers at the McCormick plant. Albert Parsons and other anarchists plan a protest at Haymarket Square for the next night.

Americans who did not work in factories, especially those who had come to the United States before the Civil War, believed that the wealthy capitalists were right in getting all that they demanded. After all, these men were risking their money to change America into a world power. They believed that the laborers, most of whom were either immigrants or African Americans, were not entitled to anything more than they were given by their employers.

American Cities Grow

The changes occurring throughout the 1870s and 1880s were enormous, exciting, and frightening. The United States was now connected from California to New York by railroad. This meant that people could travel across America at speeds unimagined by those who had traveled only by horse-drawn wagons. Manufactured goods, fresh produce, and raw materials could be transported from one state to another quickly. The men who controlled and owned the railroads, the factories, the telegraph company, the steel mills, the meat-packing plants, and the coal mines had the means to transform America from a minor country into an important player among the world's nations. But these barons of industry also controlled wages, the cost of travel, raw materials, and production. A handful of men had become so rich and powerful in a few short years that they received no interference from the government. They hired their own personal "protectors" to break up strikes and force the workers to accept any pay that was offered them.

These men liked to employ recent immigrants to America because they would work for very little money without complaint. No one paid attention to the condition of their workplaces or the shacks in which they lived. When a group of social workers surveyed working conditions at the Carnegie Steel Company in Pittsburgh, they reported:

> Foreigners as a rule earn the lowest wages and work the full stint of hours. . . . Many work in intense heat, in the din of machinery and the noise of escaping steam. . . . The congested condition of most of the plants in Pittsburgh adds to

the physical discomforts . . . while their ignorance of the language and of modern machinery increase the risk. How many of the Slavs, Lithuanians and Italians are injured in Pittsburgh in one year is unknown. No reliable statistics are compiled.[14]

The Chicago Fire Makes Things Worse for Workers

Chicago was the fastest growing city in the United States at the time. But little had been done to rebuild the city after the fire of 1871. Thousands of homes and businesses were destroyed. It took three days to put out the fire.

Hundreds of thousands of dollars had been sent by people throughout the world to help those left homeless. But the board of directors of the Chicago Relief and Aid Society used much of that money to enrich themselves instead.[15] Fewer than ten thousand people actually received any assistance.

Crowds of out-of-work men and women paraded through the streets in what were called "bread riots." Just before Christmas 1873, twenty thousand men, women, and children marched to city hall to demand "bread for the needy, clothing for the naked, and houses for the homeless."[16]

The wealthy people of Chicago turned their backs. The *Chicago Times* suggested that instead of food and clothing, "Hand grenades should be thrown among these union sailors who are striving to obtain higher wages and less hours." The *Chicago Herald* suggested that "when a tramp asks for bread, put strychnine or arsenic on it and he will not trouble you any more. . . ."[17]

When members of the Citizens Association of Chicago investigated living conditions among immigrant workers, they found three and four families living together in single rooms. Entire families were found starving to death. Many apartments had no heat.[18] Michael Schwab, who would become one of the defendants in the Haymarket trial, was a reporter for the German-language newspaper, the *Arbeiter-Zeitung*. What he saw left him shaken. He wrote,

> Thousands of laborers in the city of Chicago live in rooms without sufficient protection from the weather, without proper ventilation, in which never a stream of sunlight flows. . . . From the ash barrels they gather half rotten vegetables; . . . Is it a wonder that diseases of all kinds kill men, women and children in such places by wholesale, especially children?[19]

Workers' Rights Ignored

By the beginning of the 1880s factories again began to hire, as the economic depression lifted. Nevertheless, people who were "lucky" enough to work in a factory during the 1880s were at the mercy of their employers, who set the terms of the workday. If workers complained about wages or working conditions, they would be fired and "blacklisted" by employers—that is, their names would be sent to other factory owners so that they would never be able to get work.

No Laws to Protect Women and Children

Charging workers a fine was common in shops, hotels, and restaurants, but especially in places where women and children worked. Workers were fined for such things as coming in late, being absent without permission, and singing or talking with one another during working hours. If their work was not perfect, they were also fined. Sometimes women and children would be fined for no reason at all.[20]

In some factories, especially where women and children worked in the sewing trade, the workers had to pay part of the cost of their sewing machines. If they left that place of work, and the machine was not "paid for," they "lost" their investment, and the employer kept the sewing machine. Seamstresses had to pay for their own needles and thread. If a machine broke down, they would have to contribute to the cost of the repair. Often workers went home with empty pay envelopes.

Until 1887 only three states made it illegal for women and children to work more than eight to ten hours a day. Only four states had rules that prohibited women from working in the coal mines.[21]

The Eight-Hour Workday Movement Grows

Many workers could find work for only two thirds of the year. It seemed logical that if people worked eight-hour days instead of ten- or twelve-hour days, more people would have jobs all year long. By working shorter hours, people might actually produce more because they would not work until they were exhausted. The barons (or leaders) of industry, of course, did not agree.

In the 1860s, the eight-hour workday movement gained momentum. Eight-Hour Leagues sprang up all over the

Children as young as seven worked in factories such as this textile mill. The hours were long, the pay poor, and the conditions often horrendous.

United States. In Chicago, a printer named Albert Parsons became the spokesman for the Chicago Eight-Hour League. He spoke before Congress in 1880. The law previously passed by Congress applied only to federal workers. In 1884, the Federation of Trades and Labor Unions (forerunner of the American Federation of Labor, or AFL) set a May 1, 1886, deadline for all American employers to adopt the eight-hour workday, although most had not. On May 1, 1886, in Chicago, it was reported that eighty thousand people demonstrated in support of the eight-hour workday. There were a variety of meetings and parades throughout the city. The main parade marched down Michigan Avenue,

WE MEAN TO MAKE THINGS OVER, WE ARE TIRED OF TOIL FOR
NAUGHT,

WITH BUT BARE ENOUGH TO LIVE UPON, AND NE'ER AN HOUR
FOR THOUGHT;

WE WANT TO FEEL THE SUNSHINE, AND WE WANT TO SMELL
THE FLOWERS,

WE ARE SURE THAT GOD HAS WILLED IT, AND WE MEAN TO HAVE
EIGHT HOURS.

WE'RE SUMMONING OUR FORCES FROM THE SHIPYARD, SHOP,
AND MILL.

CHORUS:

EIGHT HOURS FOR WORK, EIGHT HOURS FOR REST, EIGHT
HOURS FOR WHAT WE WILL.

EIGHT HOURS FOR WORK, EIGHT HOURS FOR REST, EIGHT
HOURS FOR WHAT WE WILL.

THE BEASTS THAT GRAZE THE HILLSIDE, AND THE BIRDS
THAT WANDER FREE,

IN THE LIFE THAT GOD HAS METED, HAVE A BETTER LOT
THAN WE.

OH HANDS AND HEARTS ARE WEARY, AND HOMES ARE HEAVY
WITH DOLE.

IF OUR LIFE'S TO BE FILLED WITH DRUDGERY, WHAT NEED OF
A HUMAN SOUL?

SHOUT, SHOUT THE LUSTY RALLY, FROM SHIPYARD, SHOP, AND
MILL.[22]

Workers raised their spirits by shouting slogans and singing songs. This song, called "Eight Hour Day," was sung by striking workers at Chicago's McCormick Harvesting Machine plant in 1886, on the eve of the Haymarket Massacre.

with Albert and Lucy Parsons and their children in the lead. Despite weeks of dire predictions in the press, and preparations for the worst by police, the day was calm and orderly.

Would Workers' Unions Mean a Revolution?

In most large cities like Pittsburgh, New York, and Chicago, there was a great feeling of unrest and even talk of revolution. In city after city, there were hunger parades that police tried to break up by arresting their leaders. Newspapers in New York and Chicago praised the harsh police tactics used to break up demonstrations.

By 1886 tensions between workers and their bosses had come to a boil. Over five hundred thousand men and women went out on strike that year. Employers did not hesitate to use private detectives, state militias, and local police to break up the strikes.

Unions Seen As Un-American

Union organizers were seen as "wicked men."[23] One of the first recorded strikes ever called in America was in 1806. It was called by the Federal Society of Journeymen Cordwainers (shoemakers) in Philadelphia. The court ruled against the workers. The judge said that these workers were committing a "conspiracy against the common good."[24] The court ruled that people could not strike for their common interests. That decision would not change until Theodore Roosevelt became president of the United States in 1901.

By the 1880s only two states, Maryland and Michigan, allowed "five or more workers, the majority of whom were

During the railroad strike, the employers brought out the cavalry to break up the strikers. The Chicago police and the newspapers blamed Albert Parsons for the strike.

citizens of the United States," to organize a labor union to fight for better working conditions.[25] Despite the lack of support from employers and government officials, workers continued to organize themselves to fight for shorter working hours, better pay, land reform, and equal rights for women and African Americans.

The Rise of the Labor Unions

Two major labor unions to organize workers in the late 1870s and 1880s were the Noble Order of the Knights of Labor and the AFL.

The Noble Order of the Knights of Labor began as a secret organization in Pennsylvania. Secrecy was needed in order to protect its members. The Knights developed a fifteen-point agenda. Included were the eight-hour workday; reserving of public lands for the settlers (not for railroads and speculators); and laws that provided for the health and safety of workers, laws that would "compel chartered corporations to pay their employees weekly, in full, for labor performed during the preceding week, in the lawful money of the country."[26] The Knights called for equal pay for workers of both sexes and the abolition of child labor. Their motto was "That is the most perfect government in which an injury to one is the concern of all." Almost everybody was allowed to join this union. All races (except the Chinese) and men and women were all included in this group. Its leader was Terrance V. Powderly.

The Knights welcomed law and order. The group's leader encouraged members to believe that there were better times coming and that workers should see themselves as respectable people. Mostly, Powderly tried a calm approach to solving the problems of labor and management. But the Knights of Labor was not forceful enough, and while it had some power in the beginning of its life, people began leaving the group as workers' lives became more and more difficult.

American Federation of Labor (AFL)

Samuel Gompers was a cigar maker from New York City. He formed the AFL in 1886. He was its president until his death in 1924. He was disillusioned with the many strikes and protests that were taking place almost daily throughout the large cities. He thought that while the demands of the Knights of Labor were worthy, they were not going to be accepted by the industrialists. He believed it was better to work to get "a little bit more" at a time. He put his faith in working toward shorter hours and more pay. His method appealed to skilled workers, who were fewer in number but essential to industry. They included the cigar makers, plumbers, machine operators, printers, and other independent unions. Each union had its own rules and members. Rather than striking, they believed the first thing to do was to sit down with their employers and bargain together. The AFL encouraged its members to join the massive labor march on May 1, 1886. Gompers supported the eight-hour workday.

Anarchists and Socialists

Perhaps the most idealistic and the most feared union organizers were the anarchists and socialists. Although they differed in some of their fundamental beliefs, they were often lumped together by newspapers, the wealthy leaders of industry, and the U.S. government as enemies of the country. The two cities in which the anarchists and socialists were most successful were New York and Chicago. The socialists believed that the large industries should belong to the

Samuel Gompers, a cigar maker, was the first president of the American Federation of Labor. He supported the eight-hour workday and many other labor reforms.

government and not to individual people. They believed workers should share in the wealth they created.

Albert Parsons, one of the men put on trial for the Haymarket Riot, was a member of the Socialist party in Chicago. Later he joined with the anarchists. (Often people would become members of several different groups at the same time.)

August Spies, another of the men put on trial, could speak to crowds in either German or English. He, too, spoke to workers with passion. He denounced the capitalist system and preached the virtues of a life where people would work with dignity and freedom.[27]

At their best, the anarchists preached a vision of a new society where "free men and women would work willingly for themselves and each other instead of unwillingly for a capitalist employer."[28] Powerful speakers like Albert Parsons and August Spies could capture the imagination of the unemployed, the hungry, and the working poor. The message they gave was one of hope. To draw people in, the anarchists organized huge street parades with banners flying and marching bands playing. They held picnics, concerts, and dances on Saturday nights and Sunday afternoons when workers were off. They offered workers hope and something nice to look forward to. The anarchists envisioned a world in which the labor of a man or woman was valued, where people valued each other and did not need government. Soon both skilled and unskilled workers, employed and unemployed, especially among immigrants from Germany and Bohemia (now the Czech Republic), flocked to the International Working People's Association (IWPA).

But there was another side to the anarchists. As brutality against the workers increased—as the factory owners refused to give in to worker demands and used force against them when they went out on strike—the anarchists began to call on workers to arm themselves in defense.

Some of Chicago's anarchists, including Adolph Fischer and George Engel (two more men who would be put on trial) did not think the IWPA was moving fast enough. They joined the armed section of the movement, the *Lehr-und-Wehr-Verein* (Instruction and Protection Society). Fischer did not think the wealthy businesspeople would ever give up their power unless they were forced to do so.

Workers Unite for May Day Demonstrations

Workers all across the United States put aside their differences to strike for the eight-hour workday on May 1, 1886. Samuel Gompers proclaimed that from that day onward, eight hours would constitute a legal day's labor. At first, the anarchists in Chicago did not think they would go along, but they soon changed their minds when it was clear that working people everywhere were joining in the demonstrations. Some anarchists were still calling for workers to arm themselves, fearing that the police and private detectives would use their guns, but no one paid attention to them.

As May 1 neared, industry leaders began to realize that workers everywhere were gaining in strength. Indeed, on

Albert Parsons was a skilled orator and writer on behalf of the rights of workers. He argued for the right to an eight-hour workday.

that day over three hundred thousand men and women laid down their tools in more than thirteen hundred establishments across the country to march and show their support for the eight-hour workday.

In Chicago alone, eighty thousand men and women marched in different parts of the city. Speakers addressed the crowds in English, German, Czech, and Yiddish. Albert Parsons and August Spies were among those who spoke to the demonstrators. Despite the predictions of violence, the day passed without incident. It was thought by many that with this show of strength, victory was finally near for the workers.

All of that was soon to change, however, as the events of May 4 dashed workers' dreams.

chapter three

THE DEFENDANTS

ACCUSED—Who were the eight men who were being tried for murder? Were they the revolutionaries the newspapers wrote about? Were they the men who ordered that a bomb be made and thrown into a crowd of police officers? Were they "lazy louts" as one newspaper described them? Were they men who could not hold a job and were just trying to stir up trouble? Were they all "foreigners" who brought anarchist and communist ideas to America, intent on destroying the American way of life? "With hardly an exception the Anarchists are foreigners speaking foreign languages," reported one daily newspaper. "Many of them [are] unable to speak English, some of them having been in the country only a few months."[1]

It was true that most of the defendants were German-born. However, Albert Parsons was an American citizen by birth. Oscar Neebe had been born in New York City, but his parents returned to Germany when he was an infant. Neebe came back to the

United States when he was fourteen. Samuel Fielden had been born in Lancashire, England. The others had been born in Germany. August Spies spoke excellent English.

Some did speak of or write about the need for the use of force if workers were attacked. But none had acted on it. Louis Lingg had bombs in his room. He had been making them. But making bombs was, at this time, not illegal. And he had not even gone to the Haymarket rally that evening.[2]

The defendants belonged to workers' organizations. Several belonged to more than one. Some were trade unions (for example, typographical unions, carpenters' unions, etc.); others were socialist groups, and still others were anarchist groups. One, the Chicago *Lehr-und-Wehr-Verein,* had been chartered by the state of Illinois in 1875. The organization's stated goals were to teach its members about the law and to train them in the use of arms.[3] Two defendants, Fischer and Engel, were members of this group. They both attended a meeting the night before the rally. All eight defendants were members of the IWPA, which had branches in several major cities in the United States and in Europe. This organization was anarchist in its focus, yet it helped organize trade unions and was in the forefront of the eight-hour workday movement. Albert Parsons, August Spies, Michael Schwab, and Oscar Neebe were elected to its General Committee and advised many local anarchist groups in Chicago.

Although none of the defendants held a factory job, they all worked. Albert Parsons and Adolph Fischer were printers. August Spies was an editor and a skilled furniture maker. Michael Schwab worked as a bookbinder. Samuel Fielden was a teamster. He drove a wagon with a team of horses. Louis Lingg, who was identified as a "revolutionary," earned his living as a carpenter. Oscar Neebe was part owner of a yeast factory that provided the yeast needed to make beer. George Engel was the owner of a toy store. All were independent workers who, like others in the same position, saw their way of life being destroyed by the sweeping changes being made by the Industrial Revolution. Their jobs were being done by machines. They feared that workers were being turned into machines as well.

They were not opposed to the Industrial Revolution—the period during the 1700s and early 1800s when great changes took place in the lives and work of people in several parts of the world. The changes came as a result of industrialization and mechanization. "We don't fight machinery," Albert Parsons said. "We don't oppose the thing. It is only the manner and methods of employing them that we object to. That is all."[4] Parsons and other anarchists argued for a more humane way to create jobs that honored the dignity of working men and women. Of the eight men on trial, two—Albert Parsons and August Spies—were the most admired by the workers and most feared and hated by the press and leaders of industry.

Albert Parsons

Albert Parsons was a skilled speaker who spoke on behalf of the rights of working men and women. He could trace his roots back to pre-Revolutionary days. His ancestors had come to America on the second voyage of the *Mayflower* (the ship that brought the Pilgrims to America). Born in 1848, Albert was the youngest of ten children. His parents died by his fourth birthday, and he was sent to live with a married brother in Tyler, Texas. At age twelve, he was an apprentice to the publisher of the *Galveston News.* He would learn the printing trade. His boss was a leader in the proslavery movement. Albert soon learned that the printed word was an important tool in influencing the way people thought.

When the Civil War broke out in 1861, Parsons lied about his age and joined the Confederate Army. By the time the war ended in 1865, he was just seventeen years old.

After the war ended, Parsons moved to Waco, Texas, and traded his mule for forty acres of corn ready to be harvested. He hired some newly freed former slaves and paid them to pick his crops. He made enough money from the sale of the corn to pay for six months' tuition at Waco University, where he studied economics and philosophy.

Before he was twenty years old, he started a weekly newspaper called the *Spectator.* He urged his readers to accept the new Constitutional amendments that gave the right of citizenship to former slaves. Young Parsons found he had a gift for public speaking. He traveled throughout Texas giving lectures on the rights of former slaves. Such talk quickly made enemies among white people. He was called a "scalawag"—a term used by Southern whites for a white Southerner who supported the rights of former slaves. One newspaper denounced Parsons as "a violent agitator, affiliated with the worst class of negroes [sic] and ever ready to stir them to strife."[5]

Parsons further infuriated the local white population in 1872 when he met and married Lucy Gathings, who was Mexican, Indian, and African American. The young couple moved to Chicago in 1873.

Despite the fact that the Panic of 1873 had thrown the country into a deep depression, Parsons landed a job as a typesetter at the *Chicago Times*. Lucy worked as a skilled seamstress. They had two children, a boy and a girl.

The depression lasted for several years. By 1879 over 3 million Americans were out of work. In Chicago, there were records of entire families dying of starvation.[6] It was during this period that Albert Parsons turned his attention to the labor movement. He investigated charges that the businessmen who controlled the Chicago Relief and Aid Society were distributing money to their wealthy friends instead of to people in need. The society was supposed to distribute the money, donated by thousands of people from all over the world, to help the homeless after the Great Chicago Fire. Parsons' investigation showed the "distressed and impoverished people for whom it [the money] was intended were denied its use."[7]

Parsons, who had witnessed slavery in the South, compared the lives of working people in Chicago during this period of great unemployment and poor wages to slavery. He believed that the conditions under which factory workers were forced to work were similar to slavery. "Chattel slavery [slaves who are considered private property]," he declared, had been replaced by "wage slavery [people who are hired by factory owners who deny people their rights]."[8]

At first Parsons thought that capitalism should be replaced by socialism. He believed that private ownership of factories should be abolished, that either the government or the workers should own them. Parsons became an eloquent speaker not only for workers' rights, but also for workers using their power to vote and change laws that favored the wealthy. Albert Parsons did not support the use of violence to achieve workers' rights (unless necessary). Nonetheless, he and August Spies were branded by the *Chicago Tribune* as "a parcel of blatant Communist demagogues."[9]

By 1877 Parsons ran for public office in Chicago. He ran on a platform of labor reform, public ownership of such utilities as water and electricity, fair working hours, and fair wages. He lost, but he ran for other offices, including state assemblyman, sheriff of Cook County, and county clerk. He lost every election. But he became well known both to many of those he disagreed with and to those who believed in him.

Trouble came when Parsons called for a meeting of workers on July 23, just before the nationwide strike of 1877 reached Chicago. Thousands of men and women attended this rally and were spellbound by Parsons' speech. He called on workers to organize "into the Grand Army of Labor, . . . and if the capitalist engages in warfare against our rights, then we shall resist him with all the means that God has given us."[10]

The railroad strike reached Chicago on the night of July 23, 1877, and by the next morning all the railroads in

Lucy Parsons wrote many articles for the Alarm, *the newspaper her husband had founded, about working women and children and the unemployed.*

Chicago had been shut down. Thousands of workers walked off their jobs in support of the striking railroad workers.[11]

Many important people in the city of Chicago, including the head of the Pinkerton Detective Agency, Police Superintendent Hickey, and other city officials laid the blame for the citywide strike on Albert Parsons. When he reported to work at the *Chicago Times,* he learned he had been fired. Later he would discover that he had been black-listed. His name had been placed on a list of "undesirables," and no other newspaper would hire him.

Parsons walked over to the offices of the German-language newspaper, the *Arbeiter-Zeitung.* While he was there, two men came and told him he was wanted in the mayor's office. Many city officials were waiting for him when he got there. Parsons was warned that he had no business living in Chicago. When he was finally allowed to leave, Police Superintendent Hickey told him "Parsons, your life is in danger. I advise you to leave the city at once. Beware. . . . You are likely to be assassinated at any moment on the street."[12]

Out of work, cursed by the city officials, and unable to get work at any other daily newspaper in Chicago, Albert Parsons did not run. Instead, he started his own English-language newspaper called the *Alarm.* His wife, Lucy, wrote many articles dealing with the problems faced by the unem-ployed and working women and children. To supplement their meager income, Lucy and Albert Parsons opened a dress shop. Albert continued to organize workers and became a spokesperson for the eight-hour workday. He traveled around the country giving speeches on behalf of the eight-hour movement.

At the time of the huge May Day demonstration on May 1, 1886, newspapers such as the *Chicago Mail* had again branded Parsons and August Spies as troublemakers. "These two fellows have been at work fomenting disorder for the last ten years. They should have been driven out of the city long ago. . . . Hold them personally responsible for any trouble that occurs. Make an example of them if trouble does occur!"[13]

Trouble did not occur until the night of May 4, after Parsons had finished his speech at the Haymarket rally. He had brought his wife and his children to the rally, and as soon as he finished speaking, he and his family headed over to a social club for working men and women called Zepf's Hall. Friends were there waiting for them. A short time later, the bomb exploded. People went running into Zepf's Hall for shelter. Realizing that something terrible had happened, Parsons' wife and friends urged him to leave Chicago. They feared for his life. Reluctantly, he left and was taken in by friends in various cities.

Albert Parsons could have found a way to disappear. But he chose a different path. He decided to stand trial with his friends. He still had faith in the American justice system. "Knowing myself innocent of crime, I came forward and gave myself up for trial. I sought a fair and impartial trial before a jury of my peers, and knew that I preferred to be tried and take the chances of an acquittal with my friends to being hunted as a felon."[14]

August Spies

August Spies was born in Germany in 1855. As a boy, he was educated in good schools and was trained to follow in his father's footsteps as a government official. However, his father's sudden death when August was seventeen changed things. As the oldest of a large number of children, August thought it was best to give up his education, which was expensive. He came to the United States in 1872. "Upon the advice of my friends, I learned the furniture business," he wrote.[15] Soon, his mother, three little brothers, and one sister joined him. They moved to Chicago, where August supported his family as a furniture maker. In whatever time he had, he studied English and philosophy. Gradually, he began to learn about socialism and anarchism. He became friendly with other anarchists and socialists. In 1880, he learned that the German-language newspaper the *Arbeiter-Zeitung* was losing money. He agreed to take over its management. He revived the paper, and it soon was no longer in debt. Its circulation increased to more than twenty thousand.[16]

Because of his ability to write forcefully on labor problems, Spies was in demand as a speaker in both English and German. He did not hesitate to speak and write about corruption in city government whenever he found it.

Spies and Parsons shared many of the same skills and traits. Both were fearless in their attacks on those they believed were corrupt. Spies wrote in his newspaper about police brutality. Once he had a desk sergeant arrested for attacking a girl in a police station.[17] Spies exposed Chicago banker Edward S. Dreyer for trying to bribe him to stop

AUGUST SPIES.

From a Photograph taken by the Police.

August Spies was manager of the German-language newspaper Arbeiter-Zeitung. *He was a crusader for workers' rights and against political corruption.*

criticizing Grover Cleveland, the Democratic candidate for president, in his newspaper. This was the same Edward Dreyer who sat on the grand jury that formally charged Spies and the others with murder.[18]

Like Albert Parsons, August Spies ran for political office in Chicago, and like Parsons, he too lost his elections. As time went on, he came to believe that the ballot box was not the way to change the lives of the workers. He became more radical in his thinking and joined several anarchist organizations.

Spies was considered very handsome, with striking blue eyes, a light brown mustache, and wavy hair. During the trial, he always appeared well dressed and trim. In fact, he attracted the attention of one wealthy young woman, Nina van Zandt, who came to the trial each day. She said that she expected to find the men on trial to be a "rare collection of stupid, vicious, and criminal-looking men. I was greatly surprised to find that several of them . . . had intelligent, kindly and good faces."[19] Van Zandt was particularly drawn to August Spies. She visited him often in jail, and they fell in love. When the officials at the jail refused to permit them to marry, van Zandt arranged to be married by "proxy"—with August's brother standing in for him.

August Spies came to believe that the only way working men and women could improve their condition was through revolution. He studied the writings of Thomas Paine and Karl Marx. He said that he was against violence. But he told one group of Congregational ministers that he did not think workers' lives would improve without loss of life.[20]

And what about the others who were charged with murder? Adolph Fischer had come to America from Germany in 1873 at age fifteen. He, too, was a typesetter and worked at the *Arbeiter-Zeitung*. He believed in the use of force and was probably the one who summoned the workers to Haymarket Square by using the word "armed."

George Engel had come to the United States from Germany in 1873. He was a socialist. It seemed he was charged with murder simply because he had attended a meeting of the armed sections of the anarchists at Greif's Hall the night before Haymarket.

Louis Lingg was the youngest of the men on trial. He had only recently come to America from Germany, and he was just twenty-one. Yet he was an outspoken supporter of violence and also a maker of bombs. The police believed that Lingg was the person who had made the bomb that went off at the Haymarket rally.

Oscar Neebe had been born in New York City. Although he knew Spies and Parsons, there was nothing to connect him to the riot. He did not attend the meeting at Greif's Hall and was not at Haymarket on the night of the riot.

Samuel Fielden had been born in England. He was just finishing up his speech when the police arrived. He was wounded while running away from the bombing.

Michael Schwab had come to the United States from Bavaria. He was the editorial assistant at the *Arbeiter-Zeitung* and probably not at all involved in the riot.

Each of the eight men on trial for their lives held strong beliefs in the goodness of the working class. Each believed that the wealthy would never give up any of their wealth and position without a fight. At the time of the Haymarket Riot, the city of Chicago and, indeed, the entire nation were gripped with fear of a revolution by the workers. The defendants were on trial as much for their revolutionary ideas as for the murder of police officers.

chapter four

THE TRIAL—AN IMPARTIAL JURY?

ON TRIAL—The Sixth Amendment to the U.S. Constitution gives to everyone accused of a crime the right to have "a speedy and public trial, by an impartial jury of the State and district where the crime shall have been committed. . . ."[1]

By the time the eight men charged with the murder of Officer Mathias Degan came to trial, newspapers in Chicago and throughout the nation had already convinced most readers that the men were guilty not only of murder, but also of trying to destroy the American way of life. Swift action against the anarchists responsible for the death of Officer Degan and others was demanded.

The *Chicago Tribune* printed a letter from a theater manager who offered to take "the eight prisoners and hang them free of charge in my theater as part of a play, one each night."[2]

The *Tribune* of Detroit, Michigan, said that the defendants were "a loathsome and hideous set of law-breakers and murderers" and said that the government of the United States should begin to deal with these disturbers of the public peace."[3]

The *Rochester Democrat* said,

> Most of these men have come here because they would not be tolerated in Europe. They should be dealt with promptly and efficiently. Neither capital nor labor is safe from men bent solely upon robbery under the name of Socialism.[4]

According to the *Tribune* of Duluth, Minnesota:

> Such red-mouthed devils as those who made inflammatory speeches to the mob in Chicago want not peace, but violence, anarchy, ruin, bloodshed; though if there is danger of the latter, they are careful to keep out of harm's way and would skulk and hide to save their precious skins from puncture—pity 'tis.[5]

Finding twelve jurors who had not already made up their minds about the guilt of the anarchists was going to be very difficult.

A Grand Jury Convenes

Before any man was actually tried, a grand jury had to be convened. A grand jury decides if there is reasonable cause for a trial to take place. Grand juries are made up of between twelve and twenty-three people who hear testimony from people selected by the prosecution. If members of the grand jury believe there is enough evidence to proceed with a trial, then they hand down an indictment, a formal charge of a crime. If the grand jury does not think there is enough evidence, the case is dismissed. Usually grand juries meet in secret session. In this case, the press was allowed to hear the testimony by the prosecutor's witnesses.

On May 17, a grand jury was convened to hear testimony. Seventeen leading citizens were chosen to serve on it.

Judge John G. Rogers, who presided over the grand jury, showed his prejudice against the anarchists in the instructions he gave to the jury. He instructed the jury "look not only to the man who actually threw the bomb but to those who urged them on or advised them. . . . Anarchism," he declared, "should be suppressed."[6] He went on to say that although the right to free speech and assembly is guaranteed in the First Amendment to the U.S. Constitution and in the constitution of the state of Illinois, it did not apply to the accused men in this case.

> A man must be responsible for his acts. A man must be responsible for his speech. . . . When you come to deal with the results of some of the wild speeches and some of the incentives that have been publicly given, you may have to indict persons for a crime, and if so, you have to look not only to the man who actually commits it but to those behind him who actually advised.[7]

Jurors listened to the testimony of several reporters who had taken notes of the speeches by Spies, Fischer, and Parsons at Haymarket Square on the evening of the riot, and to Inspector Bonfield and Captain Ward, among others. They did not deliberate for very long. They returned an indictment of murder and conspiracy against the men.

In their report to the judge, the grand jury found that the bomb was the result of a deliberate conspiracy. Those charged with the murder of Officer Degan were Albert Parsons, August Spies, Michael Schwab, Samuel Fielden,

George Engel, Adolph Fischer, Oscar Neebe, Louis Lingg, William Seliger, and Rudolph Schnaubelt. In all, there were sixty-nine charges against them. In addition, twenty-one others were charged with "conspiracy, riot, and unlawful assembly."[8] These twenty-one men were never tried. However, several of them were given money by Police Captain Schaack. After that, they testified against the anarchists on trial.

The Trial of the Anarchists Begins

Only eight of the ten men accused of murder and conspiracy were actually put on trial. Rudolph Schnaubelt fled Chicago and never returned. At the time, many people believed he was the one who had thrown the bomb. William Seliger, after accepting money from Police Captain Michael J. Schaack, agreed to testify against Louis Lingg. He admitted the following under cross-examination:

> I have done no work, earned no money, during the time I have been in jail. I received money from Capt. Schaack, once a dollar and a half, at another time five dollars. . . . I did not know I was to be used as a witness instead of being a defendant in this trial. [Schaack] only told me that it would be best if I would tell the truth, and asked me whether I would tell the truth before the court, and I said yes. . . . I know that Capt. Schaack paid my wife money at different times since my arrest. I don't know how much; I think $20 or $25.[9]

Gottfried Waller, who was among the twenty-one indicted on lesser charges, admitted under cross-examination that he, too, took money from Captain Schaack. By becoming a witness for the prosecution, Waller escaped trial. He said:

> I was arrested about two weeks after the 4th of May by two detectives. I was released about half past eight of the same day. . . . Captain Schaack gave me $6.50 for . . . rent; whenever I used my time sitting in the station, I was paid for it; . . . Captain Schaack helped me get the job.[10]

How the Jury Was Selected

On June 21 jury selection began. The presiding judge was Joseph E. Gary. The attorney for the prosecution (that is, for the state) was Attorney General Julius S. Grinnell. Captain William P. Black was the lead attorney for the defense.

Over nine hundred men were called to serve as prospective jurors. (Women were not allowed to sit on juries in the nineteenth century.) It took twenty-one days to try to find "twelve men, good and true."

When a person is called to serve on a jury, according to a law passed in 1874, he may serve even if he has "formed an opinion based upon rumor or newspaper statements, . . . if he believes that he can fairly and impartially render a verdict therein, in accordance with the law and the evidence. . . ."[11] Several of the jurors admitted that it would be very difficult, if not impossible, for them to change their minds after what they had read in the newspapers.

The usual practice in selecting a jury is by lottery. But after several days of trying to select a jury, Judge Gary decided that it was not fair to all the men who had to take time off from work and wait in the courtroom to be called to serve. Since the court pays a very small amount of money to citizens who are called for jury duty, it would save the court money if a more efficient way to choose a jury could be found. Judge Gary appointed special bailiff Henry L. Ryce to personally select prospective jurors from the hundreds of citizens who had been called in, despite the fact that Ryce had been heard to say:

> I am managing this case, and I know what I am about. These men are going to be hanged as certain as death. I am calling such men, as the defense will have to challenge peremptorily and waste their time and challenges. Then we will have to take such men as the prosecution wants.[12]

This was exactly what happened. Both the defense and the prosecution have a limited number of what are known as peremptory challenges. They can dismiss a prospective juror for any reason. When those challenges are used up, they have the right to challenge a prospective juror "with cause." But the judge can deny the challenge and approve the juror over the objections of the defense or the prosecution.

Jurors Admit Prejudice

It was clear from the start that almost every person selected to serve on this jury had already formed and expressed an opinion about the guilt or innocence of the accused. For example, Theodore Denker said the newspapers had convinced him that the men were guilty, and he would not be able to "render an impartial verdict." When the defense attorney challenged Denker (for cause) the prosecution asked him if he thought he could "determine the guilt or

HON. JOSEPH E. GARY.
From a Photograph.

Judge Gary allowed men on the jury who had already made up their minds that the defendants were guilty.

innocence based on evidence presented in court." Denker said he thought so, despite the fact that he had already told someone he believed they "should all be hanged."[13] Judge Gary overruled the challenge.

Other jurors admitted prejudice against socialists, communists, and anarchists. One juror admitted that he was not only prejudiced against socialists, communists, and anarchists, but also that he was related to Mathias Degan, the police officer who had been killed by the bomb.[14] Another juror believed that some of the men must be guilty of something, "or they would not be here."[15]

The twelve citizens who were chosen to serve on the jury were clerks in shops, real estate agents, bookkeepers, or small businessmen. Not one was a member of a union or a worker in a factory. Except for one, all had been born in the United States.

Judge Gary Favors the Prosecution

One of the defense lawyers, William Foster, asked the judge to hold separate trials for each of the eight men, instead of trying them all together. He was afraid that testimony damaging to one of the defendants would be damaging to all. "While the defense sincerely believes that the court ought to grant this motion in the interest of justice, I hardly expect it will," he said. Judge Gary shot back, "Well, I shall not disappoint you, Mr. Foster."[16] The request was denied.

From the very beginning, Judge Gary showed contempt for the defendants. Every day he permitted "well-dressed attractive young women" to sit on the bench with him. On one occasion, a young woman was shown a puzzle Judge Gary was working on during the cross-examination of a witness. On another day, one of the women said the judge spent most of his time drawing pictures and joking with her.[17]

The best that the defense could hope for was that at least some of the jurors would be fair-minded. The official opening remarks by the prosecution took place on July 15, 1886.

chapter five

THE CASE FOR THE PROSECUTION

STATE'S CASE—On July 15, 1886, Julius S. Grinnell, the chief prosecutor, made his opening remarks to the jury. He accused all eight men of being responsible for the murder of Police Officer Mathias Degan, and of "endeavoring to make Anarchy the rule, and in that attempt for ruthlessly and awfully destroying life." He told the jury that he could prove that if Captain John Bonfield had not sent his men in to break up the rally at Haymarket Square on the evening of May 4, the entire city of Chicago would have been blown up by anarchist bomb-throwers:

> If [Bonfield] had waited until the next night, the Socialists would have gained strength, and hundreds would have been killed instead of the seven who did fall. The courage . . . of the police saved the town. The inflammatory speeches of these people decided Inspector Bonfield that the meeting should be broken up.[1]

Among the charges Grinnell made were the following:

1. Samuel Fielden, who uttered the words, "We are peaceable" to Captain Ward when asked to disband the rally, was really giving the person who threw the bomb a secret signal. Fielden opened fire right after the bomb exploded.

2. Louis Lingg was the person who made the bomb. And even if it could not be proved who actually threw the bomb, all the men on trial were responsible for it.[2]

Grinnell told the jury that Albert Parsons encouraged and described the use of dynamite in many of his speeches as well as in his newspaper, the *Alarm*. August Spies was the one responsible for the disturbance at the McCormick factory the day before the Haymarket Riot. Spies continually encouraged the making of bombs both in speech and through his newspaper, the *Arbeiter-Zeitung*. Grinnell insisted that all of the defendants were cowards. It was only a matter of moments, had the police not stopped them, before "everything was ripe with the anarchists for ruining the town. Bombs were to be thrown in all parts of the city. . . . Everything was to be done that could be done to ruin law and order."[3] The plan of the anarchists was to manufacture many bombs that would be left at Zepf's Hall (one of two or three meeting places). It would be proved that Louis Lingg made the bombs, and anarchists stopped off at Zepf's to pick them up. They were then supposed to take the bombs to various parts of the city and throw them at police stations and other places, until the city was in flames and was destroyed. "Though none of these men, perhaps, threw the bomb personally, they aided and abetted the throwing of it, and are as responsible as the actual thrower."

The prosecution intended to show the following: [4]

1. There was a meeting at one of the anarchist gathering places the night before the Haymarket Riot. This meeting, at Greif's Hall, was called by members of the armed section of the anarchists *(Lehr-und-Wehr-Verein)*. The leaders of the armed section discussed plans for using dynamite to attack the police and to destroy the city. When the word "Ruhe" ("rest") appeared in the German-language newspaper, the *Arbeiter-Zeitung,* on May 4, it was the signal to use the bombs and start a revolution.

2. Rudolph Schnaubelt was the person who threw the bomb that killed Officer Degan.

3. Louis Lingg was the person who made the bomb.

4. The activities of Parsons, Fielden, Spies, Engel, Schwab, and Neebe prior to the bomb-throwing proved their involvement in the murder of Officer Degan.

One of the problems that Grinnell had was that although he declared that Schnaubelt was the person who threw the bomb, no one was sure that he had actually done it. So he said that even if Schnaubelt was not responsible, all the men on trial were guilty of murder, anyway. Schnaubelt, of course, had disappeared. (Research done one hundred years later seems to indicate that the bomb thrower was a man named George Meng.[5])

HON. JULIUS S. GRINNELL.
From a Photograph.

Julius Grinnell, the prosecutor in the trial, charged that on the night of the Haymarket Riot, anarchists would have tried to blow up the city of Chicago if the police had not intervened.

The first witness for the prosecution was Inspector Bonfield. He described the "Revenge" circular announcing the meeting at Haymarket Square on May 4. He testified that he ordered 180 men to march to the rally to end it between 10:00 and 10:30 that evening. "We marched until we came to Crane's alley; there was a truck wagon standing a little north of that alley." He said that his men were not to use their weapons unless ordered to do so. He told how Captain Ward commanded the rally to disband, and that Samuel Fielden turned and faced Ward and Bonfield, got down from the truck and said, "We are peaceable." Bonfield testified, "Almost instantly after that, I heard from behind me a hissing sound, followed, in a second or two, by a terrific explosion." He continued, "Almost instantly after the explosion, firing from the front and both sides poured in on us. There were from seventy-five to a hundred pistol shots before a shot was fired by any officer."[6]

Captain William Ward backed up Bonfield's testimony. The police did not fire their guns until after the bomb had exploded. The civilians fired their weapons first. Ward said he recalled that when Fielden said, "'We are peaceable,' he spoke to me, or looked right at me when he spoke. It was a little louder than ordinary, than if he was addressing me. I think the accent was on the last word, 'We are *peaceable.*'"[7]

Ward told the jury that Officer Degan was killed instantly, but that six other officers died from the explosion soon afterward. In all, seventy-five people were wounded.

Two very damaging pieces of testimony were given by Gottfried Waller and William Seliger. Both of these men had been arrested and formally charged. But they were released after agreeing to testify. Both had been paid by Captain Schaack for their testimony.

Gottfried Waller described the meeting of May 3 in the basement of Greif's Hall. (Waller spoke in German, and his testimony was translated.) He said he read about the meeting in the *Arbeiter-Zeitung*. "The notice said 'Y—come Monday night.' This notice is a sign for a meeting of the armed section at Greif's Hall. I had been there once before pursuant to a similar notice."[8] Waller said that he was chairman of the meeting and that two of the defendants, Engel and Fischer, were there. Also, there were copies of the "Revenge" circular, and there was much talk about the six men who were killed at McCormick's earlier that day. Waller testified:

> Mr. Engel [said] that if . . . there should be an encounter with the police we should aid the men against them. He stated that . . . the word "Ruhe" . . . published in the *Arbeiter-Zeitung* should be the signal for us to meet . . . and if a conflict should occur the committee should report and we should first storm the police stations by throwing a bomb. . . . [9]

However, upon further questioning, Waller admitted that nothing was said about using this plan at the Haymarket rally the next evening. "There was nothing expected that the police would get to the Haymarket."[10] Further, the anarchists would only attack the police if they were attacked first. Waller did say that he saw the word "Ruhe" in the newspaper the next day, but did not understand why it was there. "It should have been inserted in the paper only if a downright revolution had occurred." On cross-examination, he admitted that he had been receiving money from Captain Schaack, and that after he had been blacklisted from work, "Capt. Schaack helped me to get the job. . . ."[11]

William Seliger, who was a carpenter, rented out a room in his apartment to Louis Lingg. He admitted that he helped Lingg make pipe bombs. He testified that he had not attended the meeting of the armed section of the anarchists at Greif's Hall. He was at another meeting at Zepf's with members of the carpenters' union. However, he did spend all of Tuesday, May 4, making bombs with Lingg. "I had previously told him that I wanted these things removed from my dwelling. He [Lingg] told me to work diligently at these bombs and they would be taken away that day." Seliger continued, "I worked at some shells, at some loaded shells. . . . After 1 o'clock he said I didn't do much; I ought to have worked more diligently. I said I hadn't any pleasure in the work."[12]

Seliger testified that Lingg was very hotheaded and very eager to start throwing bombs around the city. He and Lingg carried the bombs around the city early on the evening of May 4. "We were standing south of North Avenue and Larabee Street. Lingg said that he was going to throw a bomb; that was the best opportunity to throw the bomb, and I said, 'it wouldn't have any purpose.' Then he became quite wild and excited; said I should give him a light. . . ."[13] When they returned home at about eleven o'clock that evening (without having thrown any bombs), they saw the word "Ruhe" in the *Arbeiter-Zeitung*. Lingg became very excited and said that meant there was to be a meeting that evening. So the two men immediately went to Zepf's Hall, where they were told about the bomb that had been thrown at the Haymarket. "A certain Hermann said to him [Lingg], 'You are the fault of it all.'"[14]

Seliger also testified that he saw bombs at many different locations, including at the office of the *Arbeiter-Zeitung.*

Although this was very damaging testimony against Lingg, on cross-examination, Seliger admitted:

> Capt. Schaack paid my wife money at different times since my arrest. . . . We were not making the bombs to take to the Haymarket and destroy the police. . . . They were made everywhere to be used against capitalists and the police. I don't know anybody who was expected to be at the Haymarket.[15]

A reporter for the *Chicago Daily News* testified that he was just a few feet away from the bomb when it exploded, and that the first gunshots came from both "sides of the street and not from the police. The meeting," said Paul Hull, "was noisy and turbulent." He said that those standing near the speakers were "enthusiasts, loudly applauded the speakers, and cheered their remarks." People who were further back were indifferent. He also said that the speeches were very inflammatory. "When McCormick's name was mentioned . . . there were exclamations like 'Hang him,' or 'Throw him in the lake.'"[16]

Another reporter, this one from the *Chicago Tribune,* said, "I could not say whether the first shots came from the police or the crowd. . . . I heard Parsons call toward the close

THE "CZAR BOMB." — FROM A PHOTOGRAPH.

This is one of the round bombs made by Lingg, and similar to the infernal machine thrown at the Haymarket. It is about three inches in diameter, and consists of two hollow hemispheres of lead, filled with dynamite, and secured by means of an iron bolt and nut. It is fitted with fuse and fulminating cap.

Above is a bomb manufactured by Louis Lingg, one of the defendants. It is similar to the one that killed police officer Mathias Degan and six other policemen.

of his speech, 'To arms! To arms! To arms!' Fielden toward the end of his speech, told the crowd to kill the law, to stab it, to throttle it, or else it would throttle them."[17] This reporter, Henry Heineman, admitted that he was once a member of a socialist group to which at least three of the men on trial belonged—Spies, Schwab, and Neebe. Heineman also said that he saw Schnaubelt at Haymarket Square.[18]

An employee of Marshall Field and Company, M. M. Thompson, testified that he actually heard Schwab and Spies speaking together after 8:00 P.M. near the Crane Brothers building:

> The first words I heard between Schwab and Spies was "pistols," the next word was "police." I think I heard "police" twice, or "pistols" twice. I then walked just a little nearer the edge of the alley, and just then Spies said: "Do you think one is enough, or hadn't we better go and get more?" I could hear no answer to that . . . on the way back, as they neared Union street, I heard the word "police" again. Just then I went past them and Schwab said: "Now, if they come, we will give it to them."[19]

On cross-examination, Thompson insisted that the conversation he overheard was in English. "I don't speak German," he said. He went on to testify that he saw Schwab and Spies in conversation with the man he believed to be Schnaubelt.[20] "They bunched right together there, south of the alley, and appeared to get right in a huddle; and there was something passed between Spies and the third man, what it was I could not say." But then he identified the third man from a photograph he was shown, as Schnaubelt. "I noticed him afterwards sitting on the wagon, and that he kept his hands in his pockets."[21]

A housepainter named Harry L. Gilmer was also certain that he saw Schnaubelt light the fuse and throw the bomb.

> I knew the man by sight who threw the fizzing thing into the street. I have seen him several times at meetings and one place or another. He was a man about five feet ten inches high; somewhat full-chested, and had a light sandy beard, not very long; he was full-faced; his eyes somewhat back in his head; judging from his appearance he would probably weigh 180 pounds.[22]

This was the man who threw the bomb, Gilmer asserted. He testified that there were four or five men standing with the bomb thrower. He identified Fischer and Spies.

This was very powerful testimony. It put Fischer and Spies right there when the bomb was lit. Upon cross-examination, Gilmer now said he was positive that he saw Spies light the fuse to the bomb, and he thought he saw Schwab there, too. "I did not run at the time of the shooting. I did not move at all." But this witness did not tell anyone what he had seen until two days later. He had identified two different men (Schnaubelt and Spies) as the ones to have lit the fuse of the bomb. And Gilmer admitted under cross-examination that he had received money from Inspector Bonfield. Almost all of what Gilmer and Thompson had sworn to was absolutely false, and their testimony was later discredited.

chapter six

THE CASE FOR THE DEFENSE

IN THE COURTROOM— The attorneys for defendants George Engel, Samuel Fielden, Adolph Fischer, Louis Lingg, Oscar Neebe, Albert Parsons, Michael Schwab, and August Spies had to convince the jury that these men had not committed the crime they were charged with. Clearly, the lawyers were going to have a difficult time. First, the jury was prejudiced against the defendants even before the trial began. Second, Judge Gary was not interested in seeing justice served. He was, instead, only interested in getting a conviction against the anarchists (even if they were not guilty). In addition to the damaging testimony presented by the prosecution, Judge Gary permitted the introduction of many items sure to influence the jury. These included many pipe bombs and bomb-making equipment that were not connected in any way with the bomb that was used at Haymarket or with any of the bombs Lingg had made. Also on exhibit were bloodied clothing belonging to Officer Degan and other officers who were injured or killed. Many banners and revolutionary flags that had been used during demonstrations and street marches were waved before the jury. Copies of the *Arbeiter-Zeitung* and the *Alarm* were brought into the courtroom so that jurors could read specific articles written by some of the defendants. Judge Gary overruled protests by the defense lawyers that such items had nothing to do with the charges. Judge Gary also allowed into testimony many graphic and detailed accounts of the condition of the injured police officers (which did nothing to help prove who had actually thrown the bomb, but were sensational enough to sway the jury).

Yet it was clear that none of the prosecution's witnesses had placed Oscar Neebe anywhere near the Haymarket rally or at any meeting at Greif's Hall the evening before. Apparently the only reason he had been arrested was because he worked for the *Arbeiter-Zeitung*. And after the arrest of Fischer and Spies, he had tried to start up the paper again after the police had shut it down.

Before the defense called any of its witnesses, Captain Black requested that Judge Gary order the jury to find Neebe not guilty. The judge refused to do this. Incredibly, Judge Gary said, "Whether he [Neebe] had anything to do with the dissemination of advice to commit murder is, I think a debatable question which the jury ought to pass upon; whether the *Arbeiter-Zeitung* was published with his aid or not."[1]

Moses Salomon, one of three attorneys assisting Captain William Black in the defense of the anarchists, addressed the jury on July 31. He attempted to move the jury away from the notion that the defendants were charged with being anarchists or socialists. He said that the defendants "are not charged with Anarchy; they are not charged with Socialism; . . . according to the law under which we are now acting. . . . The indictment is for the murder of Mathias J. Degan. It is charged that each one of the defendants committed the crime. . . ."[2] Salomon continued, "If none of these defendants advised the throwing of the bomb at the Haymarket, they cannot be held responsible for the action of others at other times and places."[3] Salomon also said the defense would show that none of the defendants ever conspired to take the life of a single person. The rally at the Haymarket on the night of May 4 had been "peaceable, . . . that the crowd listened, and that not a single act transpired there, previous to the coming of the policemen. . . . They assembled under the provision of our Constitution to exercise their right of free speech . . . to discuss the eight-hour question."[4]

The defense set out to prove the following:

1. The shots fired on the night of May 4 were all fired by the police.

2. Fielden had never in his life had a gun and did not fire a gun on that night; Gilmer, who testified that Spies lit the match to the bomb, was a "professional and constitutional liar."

3. Thompson never saw Schwab on the night of May 4.

4. Parsons was at the Haymarket rally early in the evening but left with his wife and was at Zepf's Hall when the bomb was thrown.

CAPT. WILLIAM P. BLACK
From a Photograph.

The lead defense lawyer was Captain William Black, a Civil War veteran. He tried to persuade the jury that since no one knew who had thrown the bomb, the defendants could not be found guilty of conspiring to throw it.

5. Fischer was also at Zepf's Hall when the bomb went off.

6. Engel and Lingg were not at Haymarket at all that evening.

7. Neebe did not know about the meeting the night before and did not attend the Haymarket rally. In short, the Haymarket rally was hastily called to discuss the eight-hour workday movement and to give support to the striking men at the McCormick factory.

Chicago's Mayor Testifies

The first person called to testify for the defense was the mayor of Chicago, Carter H. Harrison. He told the jury that he had gone to the Haymarket rally earlier in the evening because he had seen the "Revenge" circular. He wanted to see for himself if there was to be any disturbance. "I believed that it was better for myself to be there and disperse the meeting myself instead of leaving it to any policeman."[5] Harrison had listened to the speeches of Spies and Parsons. He decided that the speeches were not much different from any others he had heard these two men give in the past. He said that there were some people at the rally who would shout out, "hang him" or "shoot him" or the like, but the mayor did not think there were many people like that in the audience. Sometimes, he said, when a person shouted out "hang him," other people would just laugh. "There were no suggestions made by either of the speakers for the immediate use of force or violence toward any person that night; if there had been, I should have dispersed them at once," the mayor said. "When I went to the station during Parson's speech, I stated to Captain Bonfield that I thought the speeches were about over; that nothing had occurred yet or looked likely to occur to require interference and he had better issue orders to his reserve to go home."[6] At no time did the mayor see anyone with a weapon, nor did he hear Albert Parsons call "To arms! To arms!"

The Rally Was Orderly

Another witness, a traveling salesman named Barton Simonson, told the court that he had gone to the Haymarket rally and stayed there the entire time until the bomb exploded. He testified that when August Spies spoke, he said, "Please come to order. This meeting is not called to incite any riot." Parsons cautioned the crowd that killing was not the answer. He said that killing people would only result in more people taking their place. "What Socialism aims at is not the death of individuals, but of the system." Then the witness said he was standing on some stairs near the speakers' wagon when the bomb went off. He was positive that the bomb was not thrown from Crane's alley, but rather from some twenty feet south of the alley. After the bomb exploded there were pistol shots. The pistol shots, he said, came "from about the center of where the police were!"[7] Even under cross-examination, Simonson's testimony could not be shaken. He said that he was an ordinary salesman who was not a socialist or member of any union. He had come to the Haymarket rally out of curiosity. He told the court it was the police who did all the shooting.

Several witnesses contradicted the testimony of both Mr. Gilmer and Mr. Thompson. Carl Richter, who identified himself as being in the leather business, testified that he was standing in a position where he could see everything that went on in Crane's alley. At no time did he see Spies or Schwab go into the alley. "There were not many people around me at the time, maybe ten people in my immediate neighborhood."[8] Richter told the court that the rally was orderly, and after the bomb exploded, he saw no firing from the crowd. Another witness, Friedrich Lieber, also put both Thompson's and Gilmer's testimony into doubt. He said that he did not see Schwab that night at all, and he did not see Spies go into the alley. He also testified that the bomb came from "over the east side, about four feet over my head. It

According to testimony for the defense, the Haymarket Square rally was orderly and peaceful until the bomb was thrown.

went in a northwesterly direction. After that I heard shots coming from west of me, from the direction of the police. I didn't notice anybody in front of me shoot back."[9]

Perhaps the most compelling witness to dispute the prosecution's case was Dr. James D. Taylor. Taylor had lived in Chicago for forty-six years and was in his seventies. He testified that August Spies' speech and manner during the rally were not in any way threatening to the police or anyone else.

> What particularly struck me in Spies' speech was his reply to some persons who said "Hang Jay Gould [the railroad owner]" Spies said, "You had better go home and learn more about what you ought to know before you begin talking about hanging anybody. We are not here for that purpose. . . ."[10]

Dr. Taylor confirmed the testimony of the other defense witnesses who said that the bomb did not come from Crane's alley:

> I saw the bomb in the air, as near as I could judge twenty to forty feet south of the alley, and the man who threw it stood beyond a number of boxes. . . . The pistol firing came from the direction where the police were. I did not see any pistol-firing from the crowd upon the police.[11]

In fact, the doctor said that he went back to Haymarket the next day and could not find any bullet marks on the wall south of the alley. This would indicate that the shots were fired by the police, and not by the people who attended the rally. Several witnesses confirmed that Fielden did not have a gun. Said Conrad Messer, a cabinetmaker, "I saw Fielden all that time. He had no pistol in his hand. I didn't see him fire one shot. . . . The firing came from the police."[12]

In all, ten prominent witnesses testified that Gilmer was "an inveterate liar whom they would not believe even under oath." It was learned that Gilmer had ties with the local police. Under cross-examination, he admitted that he had received money from Captain Bonfield.[13]

Others testified that neither Schwab nor Parsons had been at Haymarket Square at the time the bomb went off. And yet another witness tried to testify that the alleged bomb thrower, Schnaubelt, had actually left Haymarket Square well before 10:00 P.M. because he did not understand very much English, and the speakers were talking in English rather than German. However, when the witness, Edward Lehnert, tried to testify to this, the prosecution lawyers objected, and Judge Gary ruled in the prosecution's favor. Nevertheless, Lehnert was allowed to say that he saw Schnaubelt leave the rally early.[14]

Several of the defendants took the witness stand on their own behalf. Michael Schwab testified that he had been at the Haymarket rally early in the evening because he had also been asked to speak at another meeting later that same night. He did not see August Spies at the time he was at Haymarket Square, so he left and went to his other meeting at the Deering factory. It was about an hour away. He got home around 11:00 P.M. on May 4.

August Spies testified that he had been speaking to the lumber shovers on the afternoon of May 3 when he heard that shots had been fired at the McCormick factory. He immediately went over to the McCormick factory and "saw a policeman run after and fire at people who were fleeing, running away." He left and went back to the office of the *Arbeiter-Zeitung,* where he wrote the "Revenge" circular. At the time, he believed that six men had been killed at the McCormick factory. He did not put in the words, "Workingmen arm yourself and appear in full force." He told the person who brought that circular, "If that was the meeting I was invited to address, I certainly should not speak because of that line." He said that if that line were removed, he would come. Spies denied ever having a conversation with Schwab in which they discussed "pistols" and "police." He also denied ever having a conversation with Schnaubelt in English, since "[Schnaubelt] cannot speak any English at all."[15]

Spies also denied that he ever lit the fuse of a bomb and said he was never in the alley.

Albert Parsons took the witness stand and explained how he did not even know there was supposed to be a meeting at Haymarket on May 4. He had just returned from a speaking engagement in Cincinnati and was unaware of the rally. He came to speak when someone explained that there were not enough speakers at the Haymarket rally. He arrived at the rally with his wife, his two little children, and his wife's friend Mrs. Holmes. He spoke at the rally for about twenty minutes and then, because it was clouding up and starting to rain, left with his family and Mrs. Holmes to go to Zepf's Hall.

Samuel Fielden testified that he was just about to end his speech when Captain Ward and the police came and ordered him to stop. "Why Captain this is a peaceable meeting," he replied. Ward replied in what Fielden thought was an angry tone, so he said, "All right, we will go," and he jumped off the wagon to the sidewalk. "Then the explosion came. I saw the flash. . . . I had no revolver with me on the night of May 4th. I never had a revolver in my life."[16]

When the defense rested its case, there appeared to be quite a bit of evidence that contradicted the prosecution's case.

The real question was, would the jury rely on the words

INSPECTOR JOHN BONFIELD.

Captain John Bonfield was the first witness for the prosecution. He had ordered his policemen to break up the protest rally at Haymarket Square in defiance of Mayor Harrison's instructions.

of attorney Grinnell that the defendants were "loathsome murderers, wretches and assassins"? In his closing address to the jury, Grinnell said, "We stand here, gentlemen, with the verdict in our favor—I mean in favor of the prosecution as to the conduct of this case. Don't try, gentlemen, to shirk the issues. Law is on trial! Anarchy is on trial!"[17]

Would the jury listen to the closing argument of Captain Black, who suggested that the bomb throwing may, in fact, have been "done by some man acting upon his own mere malice and ill-will"? No one actually had shown who threw the bomb. Whoever threw it did so with total disregard for the purpose of the Haymarket rally. Captain Black pleaded with the jury not to act as people had before, "that whenever a man was slain a man of the opposing faction must be slain, these seven men shall die because seven policemen, whom they did not like as a class, and who certainly did not love them, have died?"[18] Would the defendants be condemned simply for being socialists and anarchists? Or would the jury concentrate on deciding if the men were actually guilty of murder?

chapter seven

THE JURY DECIDES

VERDICT—On August 19, 1886, two months after the trial began, the jurors would decide the fate of the anarchists. First, they received instructions from Judge Gary. The judge admitted that no one knew for certain who threw the bomb. He told the jury this was not important:

> If the jury believe from the evidence beyond a reasonable doubt there is in existence in this country and State a conspiracy to overthrow the existing order of society, and to bring about social revolution by force, or to destroy the legal authorities . . . by force, and that the defendants, or any of them, were parties to such conspiracy, and that Degan was killed . . . by a bomb . . . thrown by a party to the conspiracy . . . [1]

then the jury could find the men guilty of Degan's murder. In other words, even if the defendants did not know who threw the bomb, and even if the defendants did not plan on having a bomb thrown at the Haymarket rally, they were still responsible for the actions of the bomb thrower. In fact, Judge Gary said even if there was not a conspiracy, the fact that any or all of these defendants even spoke of revolution or talked about the possibility of taking the lives of people while carrying out any of their objectives, "without designating time, place or occasion at which it should be done ... the conspirators are guilty of murder."[2] The judge was saying that if, during a speech by any of the defendants meant to excite the people to action, something had happened, all of the defendants could be found guilty of murder.[3]

THE TRIAL OF THE ANARCHISTS IN CHICAGO.—From a Sketch by Louis Gasselin.—[See Page 404.]

During the Haymarket trial, Judge Gary allowed several of his women friends to join him on the bench.

The Verdict

Despite the lengthy trial, the jury reached its verdict in about three hours. It would not be until the next morning, August 20, that the defendants and their families would learn of their fate. Under the laws of Illinois, the jurors not only decided if the men were guilty, but they also assessed the men's punishment.

After the defendants were led into the courtroom, and the members of their families were seated, Judge Gary asked the foreperson of the jury, Mr. Osborn, if the jury had reached a verdict. "We have," he replied, and he handed the clerk a paper with their decision.

> We, the jury find the defendants August Spies, Michael Schwab, Samuel Fielden, Albert R. Parsons, Adolph Fischer, George Engel, and Louis Lingg guilty of murder in manner and form as charged in the indictment, and fix the penalty at death. We find the defendant Oscar Neebe guilty of murder in manner and form as charged in the indictment, and fix the penalty at imprisonment in the penitentiary for fifteen years.[4]

"I should not have been more horrified," said Captain Black, "had I myself received the death sentence. I had expected a conviction of course. But seven men convicted to hang! We did not expect an acquittal from a jury so prejudiced, but such a verdict as this destroys a good deal of my faith in human nature."[5] Black immediately asked for a new trial. His motion would not be heard until October.

The Nation Cheers the Verdict

If the defendants and their families were devastated by the verdict, they tried not to show it. Only Maria Schwab, wife of Michael Schwab, showed her shock, by fainting into the arms of Lucy Parsons. Albert Parsons, who had a flair for the dramatic, went to the open window of the courthouse and waved a red handkerchief to the crowd below. Then he took the cord from the blinds and twisted it into the shape of a noose. The crowd cheered.[6]

Newspapers throughout the country also cheered. In Chicago all the daily papers came out with headlines praising the decision. "The Scaffold Waits" declared the *Chicago Tribune.* "Seven Dangling Nooses for the Dynamite Fiends," said the *Chicago Times.* Not one major newspaper in the country had a criticism of Judge Gary, the prosecutors, or the jury. The jurors were thanked by the judge for their work, and the *Chicago Tribune* started a special fund to reward the jurors for their "honesty and fearlessness." It was suggested in a letter to the *Chicago Tribune* that a sum of $100,000 be raised to compensate the jurors for their long "agony:"

> Law has triumphed. Anarchy is defeated. . . . The twelve good men and true whose honesty and fearlessness made their conviction possible should not be forgotten. . . . Let them be generously remembered. Raise a fund— say $100,000—to be presented with the thanks of a grateful people.[7]

The letter was signed by E. A. Mulford.

Request for a New Trial Denied

On October 7, Captain Black went back into Judge Gary's court to request a new trial on the grounds that the defendants had not actually been proven guilty of the crime with which they were charged. Gary denied Black's motion, but he allowed each of the defendants to address the court. For the next three days the court listened to the defendants explain their views. Albert Parsons and August Spies spoke at length. Schwab, Neebe, and Fischer delivered shorter speeches, but each spoke eloquently on behalf of anarchy and free speech.

Adolph Fischer said,

> I was tried here in this room for murder and I was convicted of Anarchy. I protest against being sentenced to death. . . . However . . . if death is the penalty for our love of freedom of the human race, then I say openly I have forfeited my life; but a murderer I am not.[8]

August Spies spoke of the lives of starving workers, and of the fact that he and his fellow defendants were convicted of exercising their right of free speech. "But if you think that by hanging us you can stamp out the labor movement . . . then hang us!"[9] Their deaths, he said, would not stamp out the labor movement. Spies said that he and his friends were but a "spark" in the "fire" to improve the lives of working men and women.

Albert Parsons was the last defendant to speak, and he gave the longest speech. He spoke for two hours on October 8 and for another six hours the next day. His speech sometimes rambled, but it also included some moving passages. He insisted that he had not broken any laws but, instead, had been sentenced to hang because of his beliefs. Parsons suggested that the person who threw the bomb had actually been hired by "business interests" who wanted to stop the eight-hour workday movement. "I have not violated any law," he exclaimed. "Neither I nor my colleagues have violated any legal right of American citizens. We stand upon the right of free speech, of free press, of public assemblage, unmolested and undisturbed."[10]

Judge Gary replied that the trial had been fair, and the jury's decision was just.

> The people of this country love their institutions. They love their homes. They love their property. They will never consent that by violence and murder their institutions shall be broken down, their homes despoiled, their property destroyed.[11]

Judge Gary set December 3, 1886, as the date of execution.

An Appeal to the State Supreme Court

There was not a moment to lose. Captain Black immediately appealed to the Illinois Supreme Court for a writ of error. He wanted to prove that there had been procedural and/or legal errors in the way the case was handled. If he succeeded, the case could be retried on appeal. On Thanksgiving Day, November 25, 1886, Chief Justice John M. Scott, of the Supreme Court of Illinois, issued a stay of execution. He agreed to hear evidence that the trial of the anarchists had been flawed. In the meantime, the executions would be put on hold.

In March 1887 two lawyers for the defense, Captain Black and Leonard Swett, argued their case before the Illinois Supreme Court. Captain Black had chosen Mr. Swett to join him in the defense of the anarchists. Swett had been a much-respected law partner of Abraham Lincoln and had a national reputation. Julius Grinnell and George Ingham argued for the prosecution.

Leonard Swett said that the testimony of several of the prosecution's witnesses was flawed and that several witnesses admitted they had been paid by the police to testify. Swett questioned the honesty of Gilmer, who also "received unknown sums of money from prosecution." Although Gilmer claimed to have seen Spies actually light the fuse to the bomb, his story was improbable. Gilmer did not tell police what he had seen until several days after it happened, and he was not called to the inquest. He noted that Thompson's testimony was contradicted by thirteen witnesses; Gilmer's was refuted by forty-six witnesses.

Defendant Oscar Neebe's only offense was that "he was at a German picnic eating cheese and drinking beer" where someone was selling anarchist literature. Samuel Fielden was at the Haymarket and "made some threats. This does not prove that before the shooting he had aided and abetted the bomb-thrower." Albert Parsons made a peaceable speech and went with his wife and her friend to Zepf's Hall before the bomb was thrown; August Spies never caught up with Schwab. Spies and his brother left for Zepf's Hall before the bomb exploded. Michael Schwab came to the Haymarket rally early, but he left to give a speech at the Deering factory long before any bomb went off. Fischer and Engel were at the meeting the night before the Haymarket rally in which there was talk of setting off bombs. Yet they were not indicted for that offense. Finally, while Louis Lingg probably did not have the best of intentions, making bombs was not illegal. "The making of dynamite bombs ought to be, but is not an offense under the laws of the State of Illinois. Louis Lingg cannot be convicted before a prohibitory law is passed. . . ."[12]

Captain Black spoke about how the jurors were selected. He also argued that improper testimony was introduced, and that both the judge and the prosecuting attorney were in error. Mr. Grinnell had been permitted to tell the jurors that every week since the beginning of the trial "they had been finding bombs all over the city. There was absolutely no evidence of it; but he was permitted to assert that in the ears of the jury without reproof from the court."[13]

Black also asked the court to consider the fact that the person who threw the bomb was never found, and it was entirely possible that the responsible party could have been an enemy of the anarchists. Black cited *Yoe* v. *The People.* This case held that a person could not be convicted as an accessory to a crime unless "the guilt of the principal" is proved. In other words, the actual bomber's guilt would have to be known and proven in court in order to convict the others. He also cited *Hatchett* v. *Commonwealth,* a case in Virginia in which the identity of the person who committed the crime had to be identified. Finally, Black said, the death sentence for the seven men was "barbaric."[14]

Julius Grinnell, arguing for the prosecution, countered that the very nature of a conspiracy makes it difficult to prove unless one of the conspirators testifies against the other. He cited the case of *United States* v. *Cole.* "A conspiracy is rarely, if ever proved by positive testimony. . . . A witness swearing positively, it is said, may misapprehend the facts or swear falsely, but the circumstances cannot lie."[15]

On September 14, the Supreme Court of Illinois handed down its decision. It upheld the decision of the lower court. Only Justice Mulkey agreed that there were some errors made. But he said, "the wonder with me is that the errors were not more numerous and more serious than they are."[16] The original verdicts would stand and the executions would be carried out.

Once again, the press hailed the decision of the court. Numerous law journals applauded the work of the Illinois Supreme Court.

Still, Captain Black and a team of prominent lawyers carried on with plans to appeal to the U.S. Supreme Court. If that appeal failed, they were prepared to take their case to the governor of Illinois. However, money was in short supply. Four thousand dollars was needed to prepare the 2-million-word transcript of everything that had gone on in the lower courts. Lucy Parsons went on a speaking tour and sold copies of her husband's speeches for ten cents a copy to help raise money. There was also a small but growing number of people who began to speak out against the verdict. One who worked hard to save the defendants was Henry Demarest Lloyd, a former editor of the *Chicago Tribune.* His father-in-law was part owner of that newspaper. He was so angry, he changed his will and left his estate to his grandchildren. Many authors took up the cause on behalf of the defendants and organized a Defense Committee. They sold copies of their work, wrote articles, and spoke out to make the money needed to carry the case to the Supreme Court of the United States. Even some labor leaders who, at first, were either quiet about the outcome of the trial or were in open agreement with the verdict, began to speak out in favor of overturning the guilty verdicts. The Central Labor Union of New York and Boston joined in. Only Terrance Powderly, head of the Knights of Labor, was steadfast in his support of the court's decision against the anarchists.

On October 27, 1887, Captain Black and Julius Grinnell again went head-to-head. This time it was before the Supreme Court of the United States. Black argued that the defendants' Fourteenth Amendment rights had not been observed. The Fourteenth Amendment says, "No State [shall] deprive any person of life, liberty, or property without due process of law, or deny any person within its jurisdiction the equal protection of the law."[17]

However, after hearing arguments by both sides in the case—indeed, the Supreme Court allotted six hours for the attorneys to present their case—Chief Justice Morrison R. Waite issued the unanimous decision that there was no federal issue involved. Therefore, the Supreme Court of the United States would not hear the case and the judgment of the Illinois Supreme Court would stand.

An Appeal to the Governor

The only hope for the defendants now was an appeal to the governor of Illinois, Richard J. Oglesby. Not only was he a

Of the eight men tried for the murder of Officer Mathias Degan, all were found guilty and seven were sentenced to be executed. Two sentences—those of Fielden and Schwab—were changed to life in prison, leaving the five men above to face death.

Civil War hero, but he was also known for being fair and kind. By November 11, the governor had received petitions with over forty thousand signatures asking that the condemned men have their death sentences reduced to life in prison. Some of America's leading authors, lawyers, and labor leaders—even some respected businesspeople— pleaded for the prisoners' lives. They were joined by countless voices from Europe as well.

In order for Oglesby to grant clemency to the condemned men, each had to submit a written formal appeal to the governor. All seven were urged to do this, but only August Spies, Samuel Fielden, and George Schwab did so. Albert Parsons, Adolph Fischer, George Engel, and Louis Lingg refused. Then, just before the governor was to make his decision, he received a letter from August Spies asking that he alone of the seven men be hanged, so the others could live.

On November 10, just before the governor was to issue his decision, a terrible explosion occurred in the prison cell of Louis Lingg. Someone had smuggled a small dynamite bomb to him, and he blew himself up. It was his way of escaping the hangman's noose. He died that afternoon.

Later that day the governor changed the death sentences of Samuel Fielden and George Schwab to life in prison. Parsons, Fischer, Engel, and Spies would die.

On November 11, 1887, the four men were led to the gallows and were hanged.

chapter eight

THE AFTERMATH OF THE TRIAL

AFTER THE TRIAL—On November 12, 1887, Fielden and Schwab were removed from their jail cells in Chicago and sent to Joliet Prison, where Neebe was serving out his fifteen-year term. The bodies of the dead men were turned over to their families for burial. Lingg's body was sent to the home of George Engel because he had no relatives in America.

On November 13, 1887, the bodies of the anarchists were transported through downtown Chicago to the Wisconsin Central Station, and from there to Waldheim Cemetery, about ten miles west of the city. It was estimated that over two hundred thousand people either attended the funeral or stood along the route to the cemetery.

Many people objected to the execution of the anarchists. Still, the general public seemed to be satisfied that justice had been served. Except for the socialist and anarchist newspapers, the daily papers throughout the country had no regrets. "Law has triumphed over anarchy!" proclaimed the

After appeals that went all the way to the Supreme Court, four of the defendants in the Haymarket Riot trial were hanged: George Engel, Adolph Fischer, Albert Parsons, and August Spies.

Chicago Tribune. Another newspaper declared that "the bloodshed of May 2, 1886 [sic] had been avenged."[1] Even newspapers in England applauded the hangings. On the other hand, some anarchists wanted revenge. Threatening letters were sent to Governor Oglesby, Judge Gary, and prosecutor Grinnell. But for the most part, the city of Chicago began to return to normal.

Still, small numbers of people began to speak out against the unfairness of the hangings. Circulation of the *Arbeiter-Zeitung* soared to more than twenty-five thousand readers. Many people joined together to raise money to support the families of the men who were hanged and those who were still in prison.

Over the next several years, the police made periodic raids on anarchist newspapers and broke up socialist and anarchist meetings. Both the police and the press worked together to highlight the meetings and arrests.

A Police Scandal Unfolds

In January 1889 Inspector Bonfield and Captain Schaack were accused by the *Chicago Times* of receiving payments from saloonkeepers, prostitutes, and thieves. It was also alleged that they were trafficking in stolen goods. One officer in Schaack's precinct also had a large quantity of stolen goods in his home, including items that had been taken from the apartment of Louis Lingg. Bonfield retaliated by having the editors of the *Chicago Times* arrested. He also tried to shut down the paper.[2]

This time the public reacted with outrage toward the police. An investigation followed, and the two once-powerful police officers were dismissed from the Chicago Police Department in disgrace.

This came as good news for the men and women who had formed the Amnesty Committee working to free Neebe, Fielden, and Schwab. Besides socialists and anarchists, at least two members of the grand jury that had indicted the anarchists changed their minds and joined the Amnesty Committee.

On May 31, 1889, a statue honoring Mathias Degan was placed near the site of the Haymarket Riot. It was paid for by a group of Chicago businesspeople. In 1903 a streetcar driver drove his car into the statue and damaged it. He said he was tired of seeing a statue of a policeman with his arm raised.[3] Over the years the statue was defaced, blown up, or otherwise attacked. In 1972 it was relocated to central police headquarters. Shortly afterward, the statue was moved to the police training facility, where it now stands. The names of the six other police officers who died in the riot have been added to Officer Degan's.

On January 4, 1892, the *Chicago Herald* reported that a raid on Greif's Hall had been staged by the police so that they could collect money from a group of Chicago businesspeople. The raid was meant to show certain businesspeople that the death of Parsons and Spies did not mean the "death of Anarchism." Although the newspaper did not name the "prominent attorney" who accused the police of improper actions, the story was never denied. It was

THE HAYMARKET MONUMENT.

A statue honoring the policemen killed in the Haymarket Riot was erected in Chicago in 1889, but it came under attack for many years.

reported that right after the Haymarket Riot, three hundred businessmen had received letters inviting them to a secret meeting. It was at this meeting that several men agreed to put up $100,000 each year until "anarchy has been buried as deep as the graves of Spies, Parsons and their pals."[4] Over the next several years, every time there was a raid on an anarchist group, members of the Chicago police force were paid a sum from this fund.

The fund, which once had over $400,000 in it, was down to $57,650. However, the committee that had been distributing the money was quite sure that anarchy had finally been wiped out in Chicago. They did not believe the police who claimed that there was much work to be done, and refused to pay them any more money.

On Sunday, June 25, 1893, nearly ten thousand people gathered at Waldheim Cemetery to observe the dedication of a monument to the martyrs of the Haymarket Riot, as the men who were hanged had come to be known. Visitors from all over the world came to observe this moment. Lucy Parsons and her young son, Albert, Jr., removed the red flag that was draped over the statue. In the years that followed, almost as many people visited this statue in Waldheim Cemetery as had visited the statue of Abraham Lincoln in Lincoln Park.

In January 1893, John Peter Altgeld was elected governor of Illinois. Born in Germany, Altgeld had come to the United States as an infant. He grew up in Ohio and fought with the Union Army during the Civil War. He was greatly respected for being an honest politician. As a judge in the Superior

A monument to the executed men was erected in 1893 in Waldheim Cemetery, outside Chicago. Thousands visited it in the years that followed. The inscription reads: "The day will come when our silence will be more powerful than the voices you are throttling today."

Court in Chicago, he made prison reform a top priority. He became known as a "man of the people." Would Altgeld be the right governor to pardon the three men still in prison?

An interesting decision was also rendered by the Illinois Supreme Court in January 1893. In the case of *The People* v. *Coughlin,* a prospective juror had read about a particular court case and had formed an opinion. The Court ruled that he was ineligible to serve on the jury for that case. In fact, the same judge who had delivered the unanimous decision in *Spies* v. *Illinois* now reversed the decision that had been issued in that case.[5]

In April 1893 Judge Gary, in an article printed in *The Century* magazine, defended his conduct during the trial and the outcome. He did admit that "this case is without precedent, there is no example in the law books of a case of this sort."[6]

On June 26, 1893, knowing that what he was about to do would destroy his political career, Governor Altgeld decided to unconditionally pardon Neebe, Fielden, and Schwab. The governor said that after reading the trial transcript, he decided that the selection of the jurors and the prosecutor was "a shameless travesty of justice." No evidence had actually linked the defendants to the person who threw the bomb, "much of the evidence at the trial was pure fabrication," many witnesses had been terrorized into testifying, and other witnesses had been offered money and jobs. In addition, he charged that Judge Gary had run the trial in a manner that was "malicious." All eight men had been tried together, which was absolutely unfair. Finally, he noted that the ruling Judge Gary had made—in which he said it was not necessary to produce the person who threw the bomb to prove the conspiracy—was unheard of.[7]

The day after the governor's decision was announced, he was attacked by newspaper editors across the country as a "foreigner" (despite the fact that all but the first three months of his life had been spent in the United States), a "socialist," an "anarchist," and even "an apologist for murder."

Altgeld was also praised by many, including Samuel Gompers of the AFL; the leader of the Amnesty Committee, Matthew Trumbull; and, of course, the three men who were pardoned. "You have," wrote the three men, "given us back wife and children, home and liberty . . . regardless of the torrent of abuse which you knew would be the consequence of your courage. This was the deed of a brave heart. . . ."[8] Altgeld was defeated in his second bid for governor of Illinois. But he never regretted his decision. When he died in 1902, Lucy Parsons praised him as "one of those rare characters who could remain true to his high ideas in spite of politics."[9]

What Happened to the Eight-Hour Workday Movement?

For many years the labor movement suffered because of the Haymarket Riot and the trial of the anarchists. Labor organizers and labor unions became suspect, as did people who were of foreign birth. Many politicians attempted to introduce laws to prevent anarchists from entering the United States. The Immigration Act of 1903 banned foreign anarchists from entering the country, and if they were already in the United States, they were prevented from becoming citizens.

In 1893, Governor John Peter Altgeld of Illinois pardoned the three defendants who were still in prison, citing the unfairness of the trial.

In Illinois, the Merritt Conspiracy Bill of 1887 was passed. This law was an effort to legalize the principles of conspiracy laid down by Judge Gary in the Haymarket trial. Labor unions attacked it on the grounds that it would hold all union members liable for murder if someone were to be killed in the course of a labor dispute. The law was repealed in 1891. The Cole Law of 1887 made it a crime to boycott products or establishments. In many cities, including Chicago, wealthy citizens gave money to the city to build armories to house armies should a revolt by workers come to pass (or to act as jails for large numbers of protestors).

On the other hand, the Fair Labor Standards Act of 1938 banned labor by children under the age of sixteen for jobs involving interstate commerce. The law also established the forty-four-hour workweek, which was reduced to forty hours in three years. The minimum wage was set to increase to forty cents per hour in seven years.[10]

Today, organized labor unions are a powerful economic force. The labor movement, along with economic progress, has given workers a higher standard of living than ever before. Compared to past laborers, modern workers earn higher wages, work shorter hours, are better protected against accidents, and receive more benefits.

The history of labor unions has had its ups and downs. Critics of organized labor charge that many unions are too big, inefficient, and corrupt. They also complain that many unions put the interests of their members above those of the nation. But other people point out that those same criticisms can apply to many other groups. You be the judge.

Questions for Discussion

1. What kinds of terms did the newspapers of the day use to refer to the anarchists and their actions? What part do you think this played in influencing public opinion at the time of the trial?

2. Although most working people today have the right to strike, members of some groups, such as teachers, doctors, and air traffic controllers, are sometimes forbidden by courts to strike. Do you think this is right? Why or why not?

3. Do you think actions by workers such as boycotts and strikes are effective today? Why or why not?

4. How do you think the outcome of the trial was affected by the fact that most of the defendants were foreign-born? Do you think this would play a part in a trial today?

5. Several of the defendants advocated armed struggle to overcome the wrongs in society, even though they never acted on this belief. Do you think this is ever right? Do you think their beliefs should have influenced the verdict?

6. On numerous occasions when workers were demonstrating peacefully, police attacked demonstrators and observers. Were the police actions justified because people were afraid of the workers? Why or why not?

Chapter Notes

Chapter 1. A Great Tragedy

1. Henry David, Ph.D., *The History of the Haymarket Affair* (New York: Russell & Russell, 1958), p. 187.

2. "The Battle Between Police and Strikers at the McCormick Works," *The Chicago Herald,* May 4, 1886, p. 1.

3. David, pp. 191–192.

4. Ibid., p. 194.

5. "The Battle Between Police and Strikers at the McCormick Works," p. 1.

6. Ibid.

7. Ibid.

8. "Now It Is Blood! A Bomb Thrown Into Ranks Inaugurates The Work of Death," *Chicago Inter Ocean,* May 5, 1886, p. 1.

9. Paul Avrich, *The Haymarket Tragedy* (Princeton, N.J.: Princeton University Press, 1986), p. 206.

10. Ibid.

11. "A Hellish Deed," *Chicago Tribune,* May 5, 1886, p. 1.

12. Ibid.

13. "Now It Is Blood! A Bomb Thrown Into Ranks Inaugurates the Work of Death," p. 1.

Chapter 2. Events Leading Up to the Haymarket Riot

1. Neil Irvin Painter, *Standing at Armageddon: The United States, 1887–1919* (New York: W. W. Norton & Company, 1987), p. xx.

2. PBS Television's "The American Experience—The Gilded Age," © 1999 <http://www.pbs.orgwgbh/amex/carnegie/gidledage.htm> (August 10, 2001).

3. Painter, p. xx.

4. Matthew Josephson, *The Robber Barons: The Great American Capitalists, 1861–1901* (New York: Harcourt Brace Jovanovich Publishers, 1962), p. v.

5. Ibid., p. 374.

6. Painter, p. 33.

7. Josephson, p. vi.

8. F. Townsend Martin, *The Passing of the Idle Rich* (New York: Doubleday, Page & Co., 1912), p. 25.

9. Carolyn Ashbaugh, *Lucy Parsons: American Revolutionary* (Chicago: Charles H. Kerr Publishing Co. for Illinois Labor History Society, 1976), p. 21.

10. Avrich, p. 34.

11. James Green, *Taking History to Heart* (Amherst, Mass.: University of Massachusetts Press, 2000), p. 123.

12. Avrich, p. 56.

13. Ibid., p. 97.

14. Ibid., p. 362.

15. Ibid., p. 17.

16. Editorial, *Chicago Tribune,* December 23, 1873, p. 1.

17. Carolyn Ashbaugh, *Lucy Parsons: American Revolutionary* (Chicago: Charles H. Kerr Publishing Co. for Illinois Labor History Society, 1976), p. 97.

18. Ibid.

19. Paul Avrich, *The Haymarket Tragedy* (Princeton, N.J.: Princeton University Press, 1986), p. 81.

20. William J. Adelman, *Haymarket Revisited* (Chicago: Illinois Labor History Society, 1976), pp. 21–22.

21. Ibid.

22. *The Annals of America* (Chicago: Encyclopedia Britannica, 1976), vol. 11, p. 122.

23. Ibid., p. 38.

24. Lecture by Professor Jeff Cowie, Cornell University School of Industrial and Labor Relations, July 6, 2000.

25. Ibid.

26. T. V. Powderly, *Thirty Years of Labor: 1859 to 1889* (New York: Houghton Mifflin Company, Custom Coursepack, 2000), p. 279.

27. Avrich, p. 80.

28. Ibid., p. 81.

Chapter 3. The Defendants

1. "The Coil Tightening," *Chicago Tribune,* May 19, 1886, p. 1.

2. William J. Adelman, *Haymarket Revisited* (Chicago: Illinois Labor History Society, 1976), p. 20.

3. David Roediger and Franklin Rosemount, *Haymarket Scrapbook* (Chicago: Charles H. Kerr Publishing Co., 1986), p. 86.

4. Paul Avrich, *The Haymarket Tragedy* (Princeton, N.J.: Princeton University Press, 1986), p. 88.

5. Lucy E. Parsons, ed., *Life of Albert R. Parsons* (Chicago: Lucy E. Parsons, 1903), p. 15.

6. Avrich, p. 16.

7. Philip S. Foner, ed., *The Haymarket Autobiographies* (New York: Humanities Press, Inc., 1969), p. 31.

8. Ibid.

9. Ibid., p. 22.

10. Ibid., pp. 144–145.

11. Avrich, p. 30.

12. Ibid., pp. 31–32.

13. "Editorial," *The Chicago Mail,* May 1, 1886, p. 3.

14. Avrich, p. 256.

15. Foner, ed., "Autobiography of August Spies," p. 66.

16. Ibid., p. 70.

17. Avrich, p. 126.

18. Ibid.

19. Roediger and Rosemount, p. 181.

20. Avrich, p. 125.

Chapter 4. The Trial—An Impartial Jury?

1. U.S. Constitution, Sixth Amendment.

2. "Voices of the Press—Comments of Leading Newspapers on the Chicago Riots," *The Chicago Tribune,* May 7, 1886, p. 5.

3. Ibid.

4. Ibid.

5. Ibid.

6. Ibid.

7. "The Coil Tightening," *The Chicago Tribune,* May 18, 1886, p. 1.

8. Ibid.

9. "Abstract of Record," The Supreme Court of Illinois, Northern Grand Division, March Term, 1887 *August Spies et al. vs. The People of the State of Illinois* (Chicago: Barnard and Gunthrop, 1887), vol. II, pp. 50–51.

10. Ibid., p. 206.

11. Dyer D. Lum, *The Great Trial of the Chicago Anarchists* (New York: Arno Press and *The New York Times,* 1969), p. 49.

12. William J. Adelman, *Haymarket Revisited* (Chicago: Illinois Labor History Society, 1976), p. 20.

13. Lum, p. 65.

14. Henry David, Ph.D., *The History of the Haymarket Affair* (New York: Russell & Russell, 1958), p. 245.

15. Lum, p. 63.

16. Paul Avrich, *The Haymarket Tragedy* (Princeton, N.J.: Princeton University Press, 1986), p. 264.

17. Ibid., p. 263.

Chapter 5. The Case for the Prosecution

1. Dyer D. Lum, *The Great Trial of the Chicago*

Anarchists (New York: Arno Press and *The New York Times,* 1969), p. 67.

2. Ibid., p. 68.

3. Ibid.

4. Ibid.

5. Neil Irvin Painter, *Standing at Armageddon: The United States, 1887–1919* (New York: W. W. Norton & Company, 1987), p. 48.

6. "Abstract of Record," The Supreme Court of Illinois, Northern Grand Division, March Term, 1887 *August Spies et al. vs. The People of the State of Illinois* (Chicago: Barnard and Gunthrop, 1887), vol. II, p. 2.

7. Ibid., p. 38.

8. Ibid., p. 4.

9. Ibid., p. 5.

10. Ibid.

11. Ibid.

12. Ibid., p. 45.

13. Ibid.

14. Painter, p. 136.

15. "Abstract of Record," p. 51.

16. Ibid., p. 116.

17. Ibid., p. 127.

18. Ibid.

19. Ibid., p. 136.

20. Ibid.

21. Ibid., pp. 135–136.

22. Ibid., p. 147.

Chapter 6. The Case for the Defense

1. Dyer D. Lum, *The Great Trial of the Chicago Anarchists* (New York: Arno Press and The New York Times, 1969), pp. 101–102.

2. Michael J. Schaack, *Anarchy and Anarchists: History*

of the Red Terror and the Social Revolution in America and Europe (Chicago: F. J. Schulte & Co., 1889), p. 478.

3. Ibid., p. 479.

4. Ibid., p. 481.

5. "Abstract of Record," The Supreme Court of Illinois, Northern Grand Division, March Term, 1887 *August Spies et al. vs. The People of the State of Illinois* (Chicago: Barnard and Gunthrop, 1887), vol. II, p. 175.

6. Ibid.

7. Ibid., p. 186.

8. Ibid., p. 202.

9. Ibid., p. 203.

10. Ibid., p. 206.

11. Ibid.

12. Lum, p. 123.

13. Paul Avrich, *The Haymarket Tragedy* (Princeton, N.J.: Princeton University Press, 1986), p. 270.

14. Ibid., p. 236.

15. Lum, p. 136.

16. "Abstract of Record," vol. II, p. 268.

17. Lum, p. 174.

18. Ibid.

Chapter 7. The Jury Decides

1. "Abstract of Record," The Supreme Court of Illinois, Northern Grand Division, March Term, 1887 *August Spies et al. vs. The People of the State of Illinois* (Chicago: Barnard and Gunthrop, 1887), vol. I, p. 8.

2. Ibid., p. 9.

3. Henry David, Ph.D., *The History of the Haymarket Affair* (New York: Russell & Russell, 1958), p. 308.

4. "Abstract of Record," vol. I, p. 2.

5. "The Verdict: Death to the Anarchists," *Chicago Tribune,* August 21, 1886, p. 1.

6. Paul Avrich, *The Haymarket Tragedy* (Princeton, N.J.: Princeton University Press, 1986), p. 280.

7. Dyer D. Lum, *The Great Trial of the Chicago Anarchists* (New York: Arno Press and *The New York Times,* 1969), p. 188.

8. Lucy Parsons, *Famous Speeches of the Eight Chicago Anarchists* (New York: Arno Press and *The New York Times,* 1969), pp. 32–33.

9. Ibid., p. 16.

10. Ibid., p. 68.

11. Bernard R. Kogan, ed., *The Chicago Haymarket Riot: Anarchy on Trial* (Boston: D.C. Heath & Co., 1959), p. 80.

12. Ibid., p. 82.

13. Ibid., p. 84.

14. David, p. 351.

15. Ibid., p. 356.

16. Ibid., p. 358.

17. U.S. Constitution, Fourteenth Amendment.

Chapter 8. The Aftermath of the Trial

1. Paul Avrich, *The Haymarket Tragedy* (Princeton, N.J.: Princeton University Press, 1986), p. 415.

2. Ibid.

3. William J. Adelman, *Haymarket Revisited* (Chicago: Illinois Labor History Society, 1976), p. 39.

4. "Police Stage Raid on Greif's Hall," *The Chicago Herald,* January 4, 1892, p. 1.

5. Avrich, p. 418.

6. Harry Barnard, *Eagle Forgotten: The Life of John Peter Altgeld* (Secaucus, N.J.: Lyle Stuart, 1973), p. 197.

7. Henry David, Ph.D., *The History of the Haymarket Affair* (New York: Russell & Russell, 1958), p. 495.

8. Chicago Historical Society, "Schilling Papers," © 2001 <http://www.lib.uchicago.edu/e/law/legalhistory.pdf> (August 10, 2001).

9. Carolyn Ashbaugh, *Lucy Parsons: American Revolutionary* (Chicago: Charles H. Kerr Publishing Co. for Illinois Labor History Society, 1976).

10. U.S. Office of Personnel Management, "An Overview of the Fair Labor Standards Act," May 6, 1999 <http://www.opm.gov/flsa/overview.htm> (August 10, 2001).

Glossary

acquit—To find a defendant not guilty of a crime.

agitator—A person who stirs public discussion to bring about social change.

American Federation of Labor (AFL)—A group of trade unions organized by Samuel Gompers in 1886.

anarchy—A philosophy that equality and justice required doing away with the government.

blacklist—A list of people or groups regarded as suspects or deserving discrimination.

capitalism—An economic system based on investing funds for private profit.

clemency—An act of leniency or mercy such as reducing punishment.

communism—A political system that believes in owning goods in common.

conspiracy—A plot of two or more persons planning an illegal act.

convict—To find a defendant guilty of a crime.

cross-examination—The questioning of a witness by the opposing attorney.

depression—A downturn in the economy marked by low production, scarce goods, and mass unemployment.

eight-hour workday movement—Struggles by workers in the last half of the nineteenth century to limit hours of labor per day.

grand jury—A group of people that hears, in private, evidence in a crime in order to determine if formal charges should be issued.

immigrant—Someone who enters a country of which he or she is not a native, for permanent residence.

indictment—A formal written statement charging someone with a crime.

jury—A group of people sworn to give a verdict in a case based on the evidence presented at trial.

Knights of Labor—The most important labor organization of the 1880s. It included unskilled and skilled workers.

militia—The armed forces of the states in the United States, also known as the National Guard.

motion—A request made to a judge or court in order to obtain an order or ruling.

overrule—To reverse a previous decision.

prosecution—The government's side in a court of law, generally charging someone with a crime.

scab—Someone who works for wages below standard, or who takes the place of a striking worker.

socialism—A system of government in which the means of production are owned by the state.

stay of execution—To stop or suspend a death sentence.

unions—Labor organizations that work to improve the working conditions and wages of their members.

writ of error—A type of court order. It reviews a decision of the trial court by an appellate court.

Further Reading

Colman, Penny. *Mother Jones and the March of the Mill Children.* Brookfield, Conn.: Millbrook Press, Inc., 1994.

Flagler, John J. *The Labor Movement in the United States.* Minneapolis, Minn.: The Lerner Publishing Group, 1990.

Meltzer, Milton. *Bread and Roses: The Struggle of American Labor.* New York: Alfred A. Knopf Books for Young Readers, 1990.

Simon, Charnan. *The Story of the Haymarket Riot.* Danbury, Conn.: Children's Press, 1988.

Streissguth, Thomas. *Legendary Labor Leaders.* Minneapolis, Minn.: Oliver Press, Inc., 1998.

Internet Addresses

Chicago Historical Society
<http://www.chicagohistory.org/hadc>

Illinois Labor History Society
<http://www.kentlaw.edu/ilhs>

University of Kansas Education Project
<http://www.law.umkc.edu/faculty/projects/ftrials/
Haymarket.htm>

Index